W9-BAH-578

# REVIVAL

# REVIVAL

## Spoken Word
### from
## Lollapalooza
### 94

Edited by
**Juliette Torrez, Liz Belile, Mud Baron,
& Jennifer Joseph**

Manic D Press
San Francisco

REVIVAL ©1995 Manic D Press. All rights reserved. No part of this book may be reproduced in any manner whatsoever without written consent of the publisher or author, to whom individual rights revert upon publication, except for brief quotes used for review purposes. Lollapalooza is a registered trademark, used by permission. For information, please write to:

    Manic D Press  Box 410804 San Francisco California 94141 USA

Library of Congress Cataloging-In-Publication Data

Revival : spoken word from Lollapalooza 94 / edited by Juliette Torrez
  ... [et al.].
     p.   cm.
  ISBN 0-916397-41-6 (pbk.)
  1. American literature--20th century.  2. Performance art--United
  States.  3. Canadian literature--20th century.  4. Performance art-
  -Canada.  5. Lollapalooza (Festival)    I. Lollapalooza (Festival)
  II. Torrez, Juliette, 1966-
  PS536.2.R48   1995
  810.8'0054--dc20                            95-32457
                                                      CIP

Distributed to the trade by Publishers Group West

Printed in the United States of America
 5 4 3 2

Cover: Brian Walls/eConspiracy
Frontispiece: Jesse Higman

# CONTENTS

# REVIVAL

# From the Editors

This book documents elements of the spoken and written word surrounding the Revival Tent at the 1994 Lollapalooza music festival. The Tent was a place where you could see spoken word, spam eating, and acoustic performances. L7 would sometimes cut audience members' hair there. Members of Stereolab would spontaneously perform. Torment, the drag queen host, would take his clothes off. Games like Date-A-Loser and Drag Racing were there too, along with a performance art band called Subliminal Islam. Mostly, though, there were local and traveling poets and writers performing their works.

It was a strange summer. More than a thousand writers ran the gamut of adventures. People got arrested, were committed, broke up with their lovers, pawned their guitars, overturned their vans, attempted suicide, jumped bail, and basically ran away from everyday roles as waitresses and bookstore clerks to travel with the Festival for a little while.

You never knew who you would see at the Revival Tent. Producer and head Pyro Perry Farrell performed on the third stage in Miami. Beat poet Michael McClure was joined by Doors' keyboardist Ray Manzarek in Los Angeles, former MC5 manager John Sinclair read his work in New Orleans, and in San Francisco the Beastie Boys performed a freestyle set on the stage with poet Invisible Man and Fishbone's Angelo Moore. Smashing Pumpkin frontman Billy Corgan put in an appearance on the stage. There were many celebrity moments, but the most special moments came during the Spoken Word performances, when the Tent would be packed with people and really quiet except for a single voice.

REVIVAL's contributors range in age from 12 to 60. We collected these pieces mostly at the shows, though many people sent their work to us after the tour. Jennifer Finch's piece was excerpted from the L7 tour diary she posted electronically online.

It is our great hope that the people who saw these works performed live and who enjoy these works on paper will be inspired to express themselves without fear. No more silence. Find the words and say them out loud. You are not alone. Stop and listen. We hear you loud and clear.

## From the
## Lollapalooza Festival
## Producers

Lollapalooza has always been about entertainment, but with an underlying concern of educating our audience, and making them think and form valid opinions on important issues. We felt that Spoken Word had the capacity to achieve all of these things at once.

For us, deciding to have the Revival Tent was a major decision as we had no idea how it would be received by our audience. Fortunately, it was a success. I believe we touched a lot of people, and reminded them that they, too, have a voice, and a choice.

Nikki Brown
Los Angeles California

# Rock n Roll

## Fascist Fish Police — Indianapolis

Jennifer Finch
Los Angeles California

We woke up at 5 a.m. to catch the 7:30 flight to Indianapolis and our 2:30 p.m. time slot back at Lollapalooza. OUCH!!! It hurt but we made it. I just didn't bother to go to sleep last night. I opted for that "overall dizzy/overtired feeling" to the unbearable "waking up just when you get into a heavy sleep" nightmare.

After we played the show, Dave Ratt, Suzi, Double 0 and I all went Venue Fishing. Dave Ratt turned us on to this sport. All of these large, outdoor concert sites we have been playing have small human-made lakes that are used to store water to irrigate the grounds, keeping the grassy areas green. To keep these bodies of water from getting stagnant, they create an eco-system with snails, frogs and FISH. Hence, Venue Fishing!

Dave first took me fishing back in Denver and two more times after that in various other cities, but each of three times we had tried to fish, security would kick us out. Fascist Fish Cops!

I cannot tell you how many fish we caught, there were so many. We were hauling in small bass, catfish and crappy. (By the way, we let them all go back to their fishy lifestyles after we humiliated them by making them pose for pictures with us.) I could barely drop a line and something would attach itself! And the best part.... NO Fascist Fish Police in sight!

# Rock 'n' Roll

M.L. Liebler
St. Clair Shores Michigan

I've thought
About the many nights
Of rock 'n' roll I've spent
In my youth
Hardcore—

My grandmother taught me
How to rock.
She hummed Elvis
While she hemmed my pants.
She liked Elvis.
She liked him so much
That she bought me
A black leather jacket
With zippers and a motorcycle hat
Like Marlon Brando's.
That really pissed Mrs. Taylor off!
She kicked me out of the first grade.
She said I would be a bad influence
On all the other kids.

I didn't like those snotty-nosed kids anyway.
They couldn't rock
like grandma.

## Depeche Mode

Unknown
USA

God, I hate Depeche Mode!! I hate the way they look and I hate the way they sound. Fuckin' techno, dance, quasi-intellectual suicidal, wimp bullshit! They look better gracing all of the various magazine covers they're on than they do on tape and CD shelves. Fuckin' panzy-assed glamour boys, Fast Fashion indeed!! They take themselves *so-oo* seriously — God, they make me want to fuckin' puke! No wonder there's so many depressed and fucked up kids in America — they're all listening to Depeche Mode records. Their albums should come with free razor blades because their songs are nothing more than instructions on how to use them. A friend of mine told me that there is a band on Chicago's Wax Trax label called KMFDM and that their name stood for "Kill Mother Fucking Depeche Mode." Fuckin' Yeah! Right On! Now I don't know if that's true or not, but if it is, I'm going to buy every one of their albums.

Couch: Jan. 91

## Size Still Matters

Mary Panza
Albany New York

Spastic Man
Dances With His Happy Metal Rod
To A Tune By His Hero
Davey Jones

And

With A Storm His Rod Is Struck
With A Bolt From The
Holy Spirit
Making Him Scream

I'M SO SICK OF FUCKING DEAD ROCK STARS I COULD PUKE

And Does

# School

## Questions for My High School Guidance Counselor

John Colburn
Minneapolis Minnesota

Do you think marijuana will necessarily lead to heroin? Is there really a bottle in your desk drawer? Is that why you shake like that? Do you think I could make it as a market analyst? How's your garden, Mr. Hugo? If I were nineteen, would you give me a little nip from the bottle? Is it whiskey? Or bourbon? Is it vodka? I bet it's vodka. Is my aptitude test accurate? Should I really become a disc jockey? But how can they tell without hearing my voice? How did you answer these questions, Mr. Hugo? Would you rather watch a field of wheat waving in the wind or drive through it on a tractor? Are you a dreamer, Mr. Hugo? Did your aptitude test conclude "drunken high school guidance counselor"? Did you really propose to the typing teacher? Isn't she half your age? Do you ever dream about her? Do you ever dream about body parts falling off? Which ones? Do you ever dream that your forehead falls off while you're peeing and then you flush it down the toilet accidentally? I do. Would you rather watch your forehead fall off or hear about it on the radio? How can I tell if community college is right for me? Should I attend a technical school? Do you think I could make it as a market analyst? How about Harvard or Princeton? Why is your door always closed? Am I really adequate but not exceptional? What the hell does that mean, Mr. Hugo? Do you consider yourself exceptional? Do you spend a lot of time at The Friendly Tavern? Have you ever tried marijuana, Mr. Hugo? How did you feel? Invincible? Giddy? Sick? Didn't we have a good football team this year? Are you still in love with the typing teacher? Are you desperate, Mr. Hugo? Do you need a drink? How can you read my test with your hands shaking like that? Is there someone in your life? Have you ever grown marijuana in your garden? Do you think it will lead to heroin? Do you ever want to rip off the superintendent's forehead? He's an asshole, isn't he, Mr. Hugo? What school should I attend in order to become a market analyst? Would you rather draw the design for an engine or put one together? Are you still awake, Mr. Hugo? Are you a dreamer?

## Parléz Vous?

Edward Francis
Philadelphia Pennsylvania

Twelve months in a year
Twelve hours on the face of a clock
Twelve disciples shuffled alongside Christ

Fifty-two states comprising America
Fifty-two cards to shuffle per deck
Fifty-two weeks in a year

Fifty-two divided by four seasons
Thirteen is the number of bad luck
Thirteen original colonies
Thirteen pilgrimaged, if you add Jesus

Seven days of Creation
Seven Wonders of the Ancients
Seven Deadly Sins

In seventh grade, my locker was
Six Six Six
Three-headed dog, named Cerebus
guarding Hades, by the River Styx

Three men, wise and bearing gifts
Three crucified by Pontius
The Trinity
I failed Trigonometry
      or was that French?

## Test Anxiety

Andrea Cormier
Albuquerque New Mexico

How can I concentrate when I'm looking down
    into the bowl, the skull
    of someone's head
    and half the brain has been removed and
    I can see an eye attached to the optic nerve,
    rolling loosely in its socket?
        I keep wondering — where did they
        put the top part of this guy's
        head? It had hair on it! Where is it?!

How can I not panic when I go through
    folds and folds of intestine
    trying to find
    the T-pin with number of the part I'm supposed to identify
    and I started at the cecum because
    it's this fleshy piece that's easy to find
    and I've gone all the way to the rectum
    but I can't find what I'm looking for?
        I keep thinking — I used to
        use T-pins to macrame back
        in the '70s!

I try to take a deep breath to calm myself
    but I can't decide whether
    to breathe through my mouth and avoid
    the stench of decaying flesh and formaldehyde
    or to breathe through my nose
    and at least filter this stuff before
    it gets to my lungs. I move on.

But, how can I be calm when I have to identify
    parts of this dead man's penis?
    It's been sliced lengthwise and kinda
    looks like the spongy inside of a
    Twinkie
    but the colors are all different
    and there's no cream filling.
        I keep wondering when did
        this guy last have sex?
        Then I wonder — when did I last
        have sex?
        No wonder I'm so anxious.

## Flute Lesson

Christina Springer
Pittsburgh Pennsylvania

I don't have any rhythm.
No rhyme. No rap. No jazz.
I failed at the flute.
See, my mother was searching...
always searching for my betterment
breeding the top ten percent
to & on & for The Race.

She put me in a group flute class
at this inner city arts cooperative.
Simultaneously scheduled
lessons right after school, when I'm dressed
up for survival in preppy land
& off to the ghetto I go,
with a polo shirt, navy blue knee socks
and the Black Watch was nothing more significant
than a symphony of plaid pleats neatly hemmed at my knees.

So, there I am & after the first lesson
I am weak with a weekly crescendo of hate.
I hated music. I hated the flute. I hated myself.
I hated my parents. I hated the entire Black Race.
I hated white people even more, for doin' this to us.

There was a pretty dark umber colored girl in my class
with a sweetheart face who hated. She loved
catching me unawares anywhere.
Inspired the other girls to hold a jam session of rage;
converting wind instruments into a percussion ensemble.
My head, my arms, my legs, were the solo drum.
I became history. Beating out our differences.

I became a quadroon on my way to the Balls
with an upturned nose & silks swirling around my
oh-so-fuckable yellow legs. Sold in liberated bondage in New Orleans.
I became the mulatto house nigger shaking my ass at Massa for favors
& NO, my man wasn't ever shipped further down south.
I became the informant who sold Nat Turner to a noose.

I became Booker T.'s girl  accommodating

accommodate

assimilate          reconcile

pass                    passing          Passing

into the federal agent dragging Garvey down.

Darkness

white lights          passing out

white dots          passing out

   SCREAMING!!

as a flute riots in between my legs

in the bathroom taking her rage.

## Low Life

Molly McCloy
Flagstaff Arizona

Cooling coffee
and a pounder
of a throbbing headache
and plenty of reasons suffering
from lack of use.

I'll be late to class
No, I'll miss class
that first one and the next.
I'll never graduate.
They'll kick me out.
I'll never be President.
My dad will despise me for my failures.
My brothers, slobbering over
the same box of Hostess O's
as the day I left for college,
would laugh at me for even having tried.
Then I'd probably only see my busy mother
on the holidays so she could drop off
a plastic-coated fruitcake that I'd feed
to the dog living with me in my cruddy apartment
in place of my husband, a fellow Taco Hell employee
who hopped out the Drive-Thru one night
to take off with a mascara-clogged blonde
in the back of an El Camino,
leaving me alone to peel the screaming children
off the kitchen floor,
out of the sticky old beer spills,
to listen to the opera of stray cats in heat,
crying and fucking all night
so my dirty cheeked toddlers could play
torturous games with reject kittens,
since I couldn't buy them the red wagon,
but the old brown rusted one
that gashed Johnny Jr.'s leg
when Billy threw it at him,
requiring a trip to the hospital
and tetanus shot not covered by company insurance

30

so that I would have to spend extra hours
in polyester bell-bottoms
dipping tortillas into
brown bubbling animal fat
with a burnt-out, bitchy manager
with fucked-up teeth,
bent over my shoulder,
breathing on me,
asking,
"What's the worst that could happen?"

# Work

## Bad Day at the Beauty Salon

Maggie Estep
New York New York

I was a 20-year-old unemployed receptionist with dyed orange dreadlocks sprouting out of my skull. I needed a job, but first, I needed a haircut. So I head for this beauty salon on Avenue B.

I'm gonna get a hairdo. I'm gonna look just like those hot Spanish haircut models, become brown and bodacious, grow some 7-inch fingernails painted bitch red and rake them down the chalkboard of the job market's soul.

So I go into the beauty salon. This beautiful Puerto Rican girl in tight white spandex and a push-up bra sits me down and starts chopping my hair:

"Girlfriend," she says, "what the hell you got growing outta your head there, what is that, hair implants? Yuck, you want me to touch that shit, whadya got in there, sandwiches?"

I just go: "I'm sorry."

She starts snipping my carefully cultivated Johnny Lydon post-Pistols hairdo. My foul little dreadlocks are flying around all over the place but I'm not looking in the mirror cause I just don't want to know.

"So what's your name anyway?" My stylist demands then.

"Uh, Maggie."

"Maggie? Well, that's an okay name, but my name is Suzy."

"Yeah, so?"

"Yeah, so it ain't just Suzy, S-U-Z-Y, I spell it S-U-Z-E-E, the extra 'e' is for extra Suzee."

I nod emphatically.

Suzee tells me when she's not chopping hair, she works as an exotic dancer at night to support her boyfriend named Rocco. Suzee loves Rocco, she loves him so much she's got her eyes closed as she describes him:

"6 foot 2, 193 pounds and, girlfriend, his arms are so big and long they wrap around me twice like I'm a little Suzee sandwich."

Little Suzee Sandwich is rapt, she blindly snips and clips at my poor punk head. She snips and clips and snips and clips, she pauses, I look in the mirror: "Holy shit, I'm bald."

"Holy shit, baby, you're bald," Suzee says, finally opening her eyes and then gasping.

All I've got left is little post-nuke clumps of orange fuzz. I'll never get a receptionist job now.

But Suzee waves her manicured finger in my face: "Don't you worry, baby, I'm gonna get you a job at the dancing club."

"What?"

"Baby, let me tell you, the boys are gonna like a bald go-go dancer."

That said, she whips out some clippers, shaves my head smooth and insists I'm gonna love getting naked for a living.

None of this sounds like my idea of a good time, but I'm broke and I'm bald so I go home and get my best panties. Suzee lends me some 6-inch pumps, paints my lips bright red, and gives me seven shots of Jack Daniels to relax me.

8 p.m. that night I take the stage.

I'm bald,

I'm drunk,

and by god,

I'm naked.

HOLY SHIT I'M NAKED IN A ROOM FULL OF STRANGERS THIS IS NOT ONE OF THOSE RECURRING NIGHTMARES WE ALL HAVE ABOUT BEING BUTT NAKED IN PUBLIC. I AM REALLY NAKED. I DON'T KNOW THESE PEOPLE. **THIS REALLY SUCKS.**

A few guys feel sorry for me and risk getting their hands bitten off by sticking dollars in my garter belt. My disheveled pubic hairs stand at full attention, ready to poke the guys' eyes out if they get too close.

Then I notice this bald guy in the audience. I've got a new empathy for bald people. I figure maybe it works both ways, maybe this guy will stick ten bucks in my garter. I saunter over.

I'm teetering around unrhythmically, I'm the surliest, unsexiest dancer that ever go-goed across this hemisphere. The bald guy looks down into his beer, he'd much rather look at that than at my pubic mound which has now formed into one vicious spike so it looks like I've got a unicorn in my crotch.

I stand there weaving through the air.

The strobe light is illuminating my pubic unicorn. Madonna's song *Borderline* is pumping through the club's speaker system for the fifth time tonight:

"BORDERLINE BORDERLINE BORDERLINE/LOVE ME TIL I JUST CAN'T SEE." And suddenly, I start to wonder: What does that mean anyway?

"LOVE ME TIL I JUST CAN'T SEE."

What?

Screw me so much my eyes pop out, I go blind, end up walking down Second Avenue crazy, horny, naked and blind? What?

There's a glitch in the tape and it starts to skip.

"Borderl...*ooop*.....Borderl...*ooop*.....Bordel...*ooop*"

I stumble and twist my ankle. My g-string rides between my buttcheeks making me twitch with pain. My head starts spinning, my knees wobble, I go down on all fours and puke all over the bald guy's lap.

So there I am. Butt naked on all fours. But before I have time to regain my composure, the strip club manager comes over, points his smarmy strip club manager finger at me and goes:

"You're bald, you're drunk, you can't dance, and you're fired."

I stand up.

"Oh yeah, well you stink like a sneaker, pal." I peel off one of my pumps and throw it in the direction of his fat head then I get the fuck out of there.

A few days later I run into Suzee on Avenue A. Turns out she got fired for getting me a job there in the first place. But she was completely undaunted, she dragged me up to this wig store on 14th Street, paid for my wig, then got us both telemarketing jobs on Wall Street.

And I never went to a beauty salon again.

## Mother of Four

Juliette Torrez
Albuquerque New Mexico

mother of four
twenty-two years old
had a hard day at work
her boss was a jerk
the customers were worse
taking a coffee break
before going home to see
what kind of trouble
the kids had got into
she walks into dennys
which is usually friendly
but the next table over
started complaining
about her cigarette smoke
they weren't even nice about it
they were rude and uptight about it
she finally broke
she went home
not saying a word to anyone
the kids wondered what they had done
she picks up the twelve-gauge shotgun
takes it back to the restaurant
shot one complainer dead in the parking lot
you know, she said,
when the cops finally found her,
I've had it up here
with these goddamn non-smokers

## The Rolling Rock Man

Jan Beatty
Pittsburgh Pennsylvania

Never talks, never tips,
drinks two Rolling Rock draughts,
maybe three as he sits for hours
in the restaurant, wears too many clothes
for the weather, his combat jacket,
his navy blue cap, oblivious
to the people eating lunch around him.
*Can I get you something to drink?* I say
afraid to say, *How about a Rolling Rock?*
afraid to be familiar with a man like this
*Somebody already waited on me,* he said.
*Okay, good,* I said.
*You lost some weight.*
*Yeah,* I said, *a little*
amazed that he is speaking, that
he has noticed a change in me.
I look straight at him, one of his eyes
is blood, a red blotch from a punch--
he said, *You look like you have AIDS,*
*you better go to the hospital*
*you're gonna die soon.*
I felt the evil wash over me
as I walked to my next table, stunned
by this backwash of words, this bold
sickness, this butcher world that's in
and around us, *Someone please, pray for us.*
Minutes later, he started shouting at no one,
*Body bags,* he yelled. *Body bags.*
I heard the rods as I watched a five-year-old girl
stare at him, afraid for her. *Vietnam,* he shouted,
as the customers looked up from their chicken salads,
women three feet away sucked Bloody Marys
and fingered their circle pins—he heard a song
and he spoke the words—I don't know
what he saw or heard.

## The Dunk 'n' Dine

Amanda Stark
Vancouver British Columbia

gail works the night shift at the Dunk 'n' Dine
where the regulars are so regular she don't have to check the time
well tonight she's arrived an hour early
maybe she's got nowhere better to be
she says 'hey pal' to al, pours herself a coffee
and heads over to the booth that says 'EMPLOYEES ONLY'
she throws her keys on the table with a clank and lights a smoke
and blows it out like a pulpmill in dayton, ohio

she wears her self-awareness like her uniform
but by the shape her rayon apron's in...
i'd say that she don't care much anymore

gail's got a dirty bandage on her wrist
that might explain why she missed her last shift
you know two days off was just too much for her
two days of too much just made things worse
she peels back the scotch tape and peers with fascination
she is looking at something beyond the laceration
she grabs a KNIFE... a fork a paper napkin
rollin' and foldin' she gets her sidework in
but she won't leave when her time is done
she'll hang around until the sun comes up

cuz she prefers to face the darkness by the light of day

tonight she's got the college crowd
she don't like them (they don't tip much anyhow)
she passes them their french fries and wonders why
they still got that twinkle in their eye

but generally she's friendly and she'll smile confidentially
although no one said anything out of the ordinary
and when they ask her how she's doin'
she'll say 'i'm doin' fine'
(it's funny but she looks forward to tellin that lie)

the Dunk 'n' Dine provides a kind of loneliness she doesn't mind
she feels like she's on stage...
                              ...some of the time

she rattles off the entrees, that's her soliloquy
prompted by the orders she exits through the kitchen door
lit up by those fluorescent lights and all
takin' dessert orders·as her curtain call

but when the curtain falls there's just an empty hall
and she's just a beige plate on a beige wall

but there's a method to her sadness at the Dunk 'n' Dine
cuz she'll predict a tip right down to the dime
she fills those plastic baskets with complimentary matches
that say 'WELCOME TO THE DUNK 'N' DINE'
yeah 'WELCOME TO THE DUNK 'N' DINE'

and when the customer departs she will impart
'be careful out there...
                                        ...it's cold tonight.'

## Boss (Work Poem №512)

O'Hay
Philadelphia Pennsylvania

The boss calls me into his office and tells me to sit
the boss has killed men in wars so
    I sit
the boss believes that lack of punctuality is
    a moral failing
the boss is getting too old
    for the bullshit
the boss has an ulcer which he spreads around
    like peanut butter
the boss understands football
the boss does not understand women
the boss does not understand why women
    do not understand football
the boss is
    divorced
the boss has a dead father who left him several pairs of shoes
the boss wants to know my foot size
the boss always leaves those little dry-cleaning labels
    pinned inside his jacket
the boss is afraid of something
    but doesn't know what it is
the boss was cheated by God
    who gave him the head of a toad
the boss pushes his toad head at me
    and lights a Kent
the boss misses the army
the boss says I would not make it
    in the army
the boss is sometimes
    correct
the boss says he's letting me go
the boss is getting pressure
    from above
the boss says if they fire HIM
    he'll go back to flipping burgers
the boss isn't afraid of hard work
the boss has Jesus on his dash
the boss tells me to clear out my desk
the boss tells me he's sorry

the boss hands me my check
I cash it and go to the bar
the bartender asks me what I'll have
I tell the bartender bourbon
the bartender calls me
        boss

## Where the Grass Grows Greenest

John Jay Kulm
Chinook Washington

The grass sure grows green in the pasture
around that fence post
where the hired man lost his leg.

He knew about augers on post hole diggers.
An auger never cares who you are.

The flies swarmed on the sticky dark patch for days until
the rain washed it into the soil,
and the grass poured out of the earth,
dark with life.

The blood of martyrs stains this land.
Whole wheat insurance claims
thinking they colored the grass green
by their suffering.

The grass grows tall on the sweat
dripping from the frontal lobes
of a family farm dynasty;
tall over the acres,
tall and green.
But greenest around that place where
the auger pulled bone from bone,
and flesh from flesh,
Leg from hired man.

He was settled into the hospital
when we stuck a railroad tie into the hole
and finished his job.
The grass sure grows green there.

## These Hands

Justin Welborn
Rex Georgia

These hands are dry and cracked with running scars,
singing of hot, wood carrying days.
I love my calluses — they tell stories
that I myself can't even recall.
Bits of dry flesh or ragged fingernails, dirty
from the attention they lack,
remind me of how soft, and ruddy these crevasse scarred palms
used to be, when they ran quivering over supple faces of women
that have long ago put me out of their thoughts.
How could I have known
these ten crunching, popping digits
could ever make these eyes see the man outside,
that the soul could never find within?
There are many memories in this life of mine
that only these grubby hands can remember.
Their words are as rough as a gnarled fist —
and valleys of skin hide memories collected
from a life span of service.

# Altered States

## When We Get There, We'll Know

Jacob Schulze
Austin Texas

we didn't trip the light fantastic

we ate that motherfucker
and touching the pacific to my lips on that sixty-five
degree afternoon
(poet and drag queen in tow)
i tasted a syringe
and i knew that i had made it
i could do anything

we didn't trip the light fantastic
we gave it the beating of its life
and careening down lombard
left then
            right
then left again and
            right
laughing like madmen and yelling at pedestrians
and asking where we were and soliciting fart jokes from
asians with cameras and generally being assholes
i knew that i was here
that i could do anything

we didn't trip the light fantastic
we made it trivial
and at the art institute we stood on the roof
sidestepping broken plaster torso molds
and steel cables and footprints and
we stared at alcatraz
the rock
and we made clint eastwood jokes and we remembered
that scorpions video and i put plastic forks over my eyes
and it was good for a laugh
standing under the diego rivera fresco
                turning
cataloguing the blue heads that dotted the canvases on the
walls calculating the distance from ceiling to finished wood
        turning
and she was there behind me
quiet mouth agape
slackjawed and certain she wanted to say "fuck"
in amazement, in awe, but somehow it didn't fit

it was easier to be
at last quiet
and as the laughter left the room on stupid feet
and the man on the wall in the white suit like stone
like bone he was so quiet and in that one moment i realized
i knew
that i didn't need you
i could do anything

we didn't trip the light fantastic
we chewed it up and spit it out
we made no apologies to tennessee
and from a payphone on divisadero i rubbed it in
and ate thai food and then we started laughing again
between the pints of anchor steam and the drunken midnight
of the golden gate or the even more drunken midday of the
glass house with the flowers and the buffalo
crammed tight inside a cavalier in chinatown
in little italy

on castro where the queers frolic and
harvey milk has a library (there is a backhanded justice in this world)
south on the 101 towards san jose in the carpool lane haulin
ass giggling like a girlscout troop on loads of acid scanning
the radio for that perfect platinum pop
that would be the theme for the rest of our lives
not finding it and cursing the music industry for not
obliging us on our perfect twelve hour grab and go jaunt
and later
dead weight on either side of me as the lines on the road
screamed past
running together
connecting this freeway to
that freeway to another freeway
which would ultimately bring me
back to you
(whom i didn't need anymore)
and i knew then as i suppose i had known all along
that i could do anything.

we didn't trip the light fantastic
we ate that motherfucker
it gave us an inch and we drove it
one mile
into the ground.

## LA Weekly Goes to France

David Fewster
Seattle Washington

Michael Ventura went to Paris
To sit in the bathtub where Jim Morrison died
Because that's the kind of guy he is
Slamming shots of tequila and
Smoking Gauloise-Bleu's by the handful
He fills the tub until the water reaches his chin
Screaming "Go, baby, go
Break on through to the other side"
Knowing that with a mere dip of the head
He could crash that barrier and join Jim
And read him the essay on "Dionysian Archetypes & the MTV Generation"
That he had written that afternoon on Baudelaire's tombstone
While drinking vin rouge and smoking hashish
That he had bought early that morning from a young Arab dealer
Outside the building where Modigliani's wife
Leapt to her death, all the while
Remembering with regret the night before when
He had tried to sleep in the room where Oscar Wilde
Suffered his massive cerebral hemorrhage,
Shooting brains, blood, pus and mucus out of every orifice
In front of terrified onlookers
But someone had rented it out first
Some goddamn little poseur, no doubt,
And then and there Michael wrote an article
"Those Goddamn Mealy-Mouthed Pathetic Empty-Headed Little
Poseurs
Without Lives of Their Own Who Get Vicarious
Kicks Out of Renting Rooms Where Famous Iconoclasts Have
Died and Make It Almost Impossible for Me to Get Reservations There"
Which will be coming out in *The New Yorker* later this year
Because right after he finished it he ran into Tina Brown
Sitting in a little cafe in Montmartre
At the table where Verlaine puked his liver out
When Robert Bly came over,
Having spent the day in the hotel where Strindberg went mad
And he and Michael started a dialogue on suicide
Each hoping the other would commit it first
But, unfortunately, they knew each other only too well
So the conversation will be published in book form
By St. Martin's Press this fall.

Back in the bathtub,
Michael Ventura blows bubbles through his nose
And makes little humming noises,
Pretending he's a speedboat.
The moment of danger is past.
His only regret is
That he forgot to take off his street clothes
Before he turned on the tap.

## Smoke Throat Jimmy Singing the Drunk Man's Blues

Jimmy Jazz
San Diego California

Showed up drunk
to my A.A. meeting
eleven guys with a problem just like mine
We smoke packs of cigarettes
shades pulled low like sleepy eyelids shutting
telling sunken tales bout
rotting liver
shakin' hands
and the last blank spot.
I listen without speaking. Until...
My turn?
A pretty thought of alcohol
jumps up to my slurrrr tongue
disguised as a partygirl
with open smile
free floating in my brain
like the disappearing landscape
in front of the wheel,
with big "I understand honey" eyes
and lips too busy waiting for a kiss
to speak truth bout what she sees inside.
        Instead of "My name is Jimmy Jazz
and I'm an alcoholic,"
I said, "I'm Jimmy Jazz and
I l-o-o-o-o-ve to drink.
Beer clouds my brain
It stops the think,
I love to be drunk
on words and women.
(my voice gets creepy here, it crouches)
Drunk where music is a spinning cell
in my vein and brain jail,
spinning me
another tale of the low road
to high times and
I don't care if I sleep through the sunrise
as long as the moon shines
and the city lights blaze on the dark bay water

53

and time
can slip way through the bottle noose
to the sewer stomach of street sleeping sore whores
as long as the bass beat drum hump ferments into the jang jang guitar slang
under the scratchy throat whine in the downtown jump joint.
    I wanted them to think I was crazy, different, possessed by spirits, but eleven
heads nodded
and the next mouth opened to speak.

## Telephone Talk

Adeena Karasick
Ontario Canada

Can't get me no
Serotonin

Zygote cycoso ogle entropic amyl oxide
Mandala aztek. Double dipped quad sep
Dyazipan dose.

     an' i wanna go

snow boardin' under / the silver haze
northern lights. amarillo mellow swell. snow. blow
crystall cake kilo. honey slack gum slide. Gone

DOWNTOWN
                  Releases seizes de ceases
zones of hysteresis
restorying these extasies.
Keeps on *reisen* –
A synechdoche deictic addicted
dex indika mesc. scarred
in the gashes of coagulent traces

Do ya do ya do ya wanna
Base it. Space cakes wasted baked
Hydro skunk Bud shake. Kick some buzz
bunk bong balloon bong
an' i'm burnin'

                  So, *insert here* i sd
                  As insinuant sinews solypse: a
                  threnody already. An
                  anachronistic massacre
                  or an aneurysm mannerism

                  Put it in/ Put it in put / it in me
As affix affects a fix in flux. A flex of eschers. Keef
sticks Double barrel purple mics.
green gone paralytic harry bob cid conrad gone
but we're *back in black*

Lysergic spliff speedball, gone
triple sep ampheta
button gum tapes. Gone.
Pey otis dead and gone
Treebark slab. tab. trip floyd
Gone. Meperodine adrenelin derm demoral, gone
Tab dose. sheet page gum meth slab gone

Just say $N_2O$


psylysiban an' i'm looking for
Jesus Gone

Friction pivots panoply snap crackle pop
sugar smack snack crack
Anachrony pack

      slack —

Rim cut cicatric edge
ledger ram slide vacant wedge
apotheoptic apex crank kind bud
kinda. "kine not kin or kind"
coined in kind 'cuz

        I BELIEVE IN MIRACLES

## 56 Reasons To Go Downtown

Iris Berry
Van Nuys California

Johnny Thunders did it
because Lenny Bruce did it
Honey did it too.

Because Art Pepper did it,
he did it cause Charlie Parker did it.
Look at Keith Richards.
I'm a sensitive artist too.
Yeah I'm a rebel
and the scene's really dead.
And I can't afford to go to Europe this summer.
And I wanna buck the fitness kick.
And private property is really an outmoded concept.
Because I like hanging out in Pawn Shops.
Because I like losing friends and meeting scum.
Anyway it's all society's fault
you know Darby Crash, Sid and Nancy.
Look, your boyfriend does it
your girlfriend does it.
If I wanna sleep on the bathroom floor,
if I wanna sleep in my breakfast,
if I wanna sleep in my dinner
and if I wanna die watching TV,
it's my business (so dignified).
And besides I've got it all under control.
I do it only twice a week at the most,
so quit hassling me.

It's rock 'n' roll,
it's the Rolling Stones
and didn't Edie Sedgwick look so cool in *Ciao Manhattan?*
She was out on the edge
and I like being out on the edge.
Just like Burroughs
just like Thunders, yeah Johnny Thunders did it.
Look I know I'm propping up 3rd world dictatorships
but I'm not hurting anyone else.
I'm on methadone
and I haven't fixed in a week
so quit hassling me
I've got it all under control.

## For The Game

Cindy Wheeler
Tampa Florida

And when I got back to the house he asked
if I was hungry and I said, "well, yeah, kind of,
what do you have?" and he said, "soda crackers
with LSD laced mayonnaise." Only he
forgot to mention the LSD part...

The newsprint fades from the paper
Everything is written in invisible ink
Every word that's spoken sounds like
spanglaneseian and the spangled banner
is black like a hole, on the ground
trying hard not to be
the piece of cloth that is
and I should have been told that
I really should carry a gun.
I have been told that
I am living in a "modern civilization,"
and I will say that for the game and
the championship, Bob,
I'll wager all the money, all $5378.00 dollars,
that the preceding statement is false.
I'll bet double or nothing, Mr. Eubanks.
I'll put my head into boiling water,
I'll stick my favorite cat into the microwave,
I'll run down the man I love with a
1978 Monte Carlo. I'll break a kitchen knife
off in his cold, cold heart. I'll smother five
of my six children with a pillow just for some
peace and quiet. I'll start smoking crack until
I'm sucked empty. I'll walk with the walking dead.
I'll sleep with a gun under my pillow,
with a gun between my legs,
because this is the way I sleep in a modern civilization,
never dreaming, always waking
from a light half sleep with a stiff neck
and a skewed view,
my head turned sideways
until my neck snaps, and reality is shifted
onto its side and there is nothing left
but broken glass, photographs of people
I don't know, and bullets under my feet.

# Family

## Crumbs

Hal Sirowitz
Queens New York

Don't eat any food in your room,
Mother said. You'll get more bugs.
They depend on people like you.
Otherwise, they would starve.
But who do you want to make happy,
your mother or a bunch of ants?
What have they done for you?
Nothing. They have no feelings.
They'll eat your candy. Yet
you treat them better than you treat me.
You keep feeding them
But you never offer me anything.

## Ruby's First Word
(Baba is everywhere)

Sunfrog
Detroit Michigan

The universe is baba
baba explains the universe
why do they call
it baby talk?
babababababababababababa
baba more dada
than daddy can imagine
baba not bubba
but wet butt is
as much baba as
dry booty is baba

hungry is baba
thirsty is baba
ravenous or completely
blissfully satiated is baba
baba is bathed
baba is dirty
baba is delicious banana
baba is dirty rotten baby vomit
baba is
but what is not baba, baby?
Mommy is baba
Daddy is baba
baba *is* baba
a bloody baby finger
boo boo is baba
my hungry heart
hoping for fewer
boo boos is baba

riding in the stroller is baba
taking a bath is baba
singing baba is baba
drinking milky is baba
sucking on everything
hard & shiny is baba
please is baba

thank you is baba
ecstatic baba
erratic baba
emphatic baba
gymnastic baba

this poem is baba
your response
to this poem is baba
baba is absolute truth
baba is bullshit
baba is baby
baba is you
baba is me
baba is Ruby
Ruby is baba
Baba
is Ruby's first word

## Cowboy Jeb

Lisa Martinovic
Fayetteville Arkansas

They called him Cowboy Jeb and he liked that
He'd done lots of cowboyin
rode his uncle's herd
ripped the nuts offa bulls
and built the best barbed wire fences of any man in the county,
that's right
But cowboy was only part true, cuz before all that
he was a hillbilly, like his daddy and grandaddy and on back
five generations on the mountain
goin back to Cherokee days
When Jeb was growin up 30, 40 years ago
there weren't no runnin water
and nothin but a shared outhouse to crap in
and he sez that if ya didn't grow it or shoot it,
it didn't get et
Yeah, ole Jeb was a hillbilly all right
and he said he liked that
but he knew not everybody liked that
Lotta folks thought he was white trash
never would say it to his face no how
iffen they did Jeb mighta shot em with the rifle he uses for squirrel,
same as his daddy
or maybe rearrange their face with a barbed wire whip
like his daddy never used
like the one he tried to get his son to use
on Halloween
Trick or treat. . . or else, Jeb taught him
and he laughed that crazy laugh that makes folks wonder
But young Jasper's got a sensitive streak
and barbed wire whips ain't his nature
cept inasmuch as they're his daddy's
and he does so love his daddy
wants to be just like his daddy
until daddy yells like to kill young Jasper
and Jasper cries cuz he don't want his daddy to leave
like his mama done did when he was 5
and his daddy hates it when he cries
and tells him to be a man
but young Jasper he's got that sensitive streak

64

and he writes poems about exploding houses
and draws weird pictures with crosses and vampires
and Jeb doesn't understand
but he does love his son
he hates to yell at Jasper
but he can't rein it in once he starts to boilin
Now, Jasper's a real good student
nuff to make his daddy proud
but he wets the bed at night
like his daddy did
and he craps his pants at school
but he don't tell nobody
he just keeps on playin and studying
payin no mind to the gooey stink oozin in his pants
Jasper don't know why
it just happens
and Jeb don't yell when he smells young Jasper come home from school
he's quiet when he puts the pants in the washer with extra soap
best to just ignore the whole thing
cuz he don't know what to do anyway
and he's scared
But no matter what he does with young Jasper
he figgers even still he's done a damn sight better than his daddy
who beat the shit outta him every goddamn day
til Jeb got big enough to whup the old man
Jeb's daddy went away with his bottle
and never came back
And Jeb still lives down the mountain from his mama
who couldn't save him all his life
so now he saves her
And Jeb's ex-girlfriend who got herself an education
says Jeb really hates all women
cuz his mama never did protect him
and ole Jeb sez that just smells like Yankee thinkin
and he won't have none of it
so he keeps rescuing his mama
from husband number 3
the boozehound with a black widow tattooed on the head of his dick
and he keeps lookin to bury his face in
women with little titties and white cotton panties
like his mama
and he don't see nothin wrong with that and if you do
you best keep it to yourself

## La Letty

Michele Serros
Culver City California

Her steady hand
outlines inside bottom eyelid,
thick
darkening to deep velvet black.
A finishing touch
ends sixty minute routine
for this raccoon eyed beauty
Turning from the mirror
she says:
"You know what you are?
     A Chicana Falsa."

"MECHA don't mean shit,
and that sloppy Spanish of yours
will never get you any discount at Bob's market."

"HOMOGENIZED HISPANIC,
that's what you are."

She
had once been "Leticia,"
"Tish" for short
but now
only two weeks into junior high,
She is "La Letty"
*y que*
*no mas.*

Taught me
years ago,
how to ride a bike
Doesn't matter now
Chevy Impalas snatch
her from school,
Mexican Cadillacs
low and slow,
done up in candy paint, metal flake
chrome-plated spoke rims
glistening,

Young boys
in hair nets and Dickies
fingers dipped in Old English ink
controlled
chained steering wheels
and La Letty.
Steered her
away from me,
my sister, best friend.
And she fell for them,
for it,
the whole creased-khaki
pressed-flannel
medallion-wearing scene.


Every night
after dinner was done
TV clicked off
in Holly Hobbie haven
my naked lids closed
as I listened for
soft car hum
copycat teenage laughter
faint oldies station...
waiting
and waiting
for Tish
       to come home.

## Sor Juana Inez de la Cruz

Daniel Solis
Asheville North Carolina

Sor Juana Inez de la Cruz
your name spoken aloud
in Boston
to your bones asleep
in the tropics
to your soul
spinning sky blue arcs
like the wooden tops
you set tracking through the flour
Sor Juana Inez de la Cruz
your name spoken aloud
in Dallas
as my mother
scolds bookstore
salesclerk boys
who don't know
the difference
between a biography
and a bibliography
and a book of poetry
Sor Juana Inez de la Cruz
a woman playing
a man's game
of sonnets and
paper and ink
with a woman's wisdom
Gongoras prodigy
and rival
firing images emotions
you somehow knew
would survive
Sor Juana Inez de la Cruz
your name spoken aloud
at a Boston
winter cold bus stop
set free in this
three hundred years later air
I don't shout it

but if I could
catch and scatter
the notes from
my throat
I would certainly sing it
Sor Juana Inez de la Cruz

# The Beyond

## Angels

Van Horgen
Minneapolis Minnesota

There are angels
descended to this Earth.

They watch, waiting
for signs of God,

but I have none.
I know nothing I do

is good enough.
The angels take all,

smug in their wings.
They make a man

do bad, as if bad
were all that's left

I can call my own.
I steal cardboard

and wing myself
off steps at the Basilica

I go nowhere, except
down like angels.

## Crowned
*for Kurt Cobain*

Lisa Buscani
Chicago Illinois

The photonegative afterworld
is not what he expected.

The ground is white with lack of life,
ice-like trees swollen with ghost fruit
and soundless rivers of watered memory
that lap up the few thoughts he brought with him.
The door to our world
beats and throbs blueblack
from the sloppy endings shotguns make,
its frame buckling under the burden of an untimely exit.

He is looking for his word.
It is a word with weight greater than "friend,"
weight greater than "lover,"
greater than "daddy,"
which we'll never understand
but still
it is the word of respite,
balm in this Iliad,
to help him find the room he needs,
to help him shoulder the dead weight of blame,
to help him hold down lunch.

To find his word,
he must find his angel.

His angel,
black taffeta wings
muscling a tough yet gracious spread
from the back of a pale, exhausted housedress,
her gender muted by a binding all-father,
her fine hair losing track of its color,
her lips with a blush that won't stay put,
her NaNa-shod legs lifeless because
she
was meant to fly.

His angel
half-holds his word
in her split ribbon mouth like a pearl
forcing her cello alto around it,
sweet wet washing it with her tongue,
waiting for the day
when she can speak and heal, yes
speak and heal.

And he stands before her
tangle of rhyme and scream,
fraught with the cost of things,
taught through the shoulders with nuisance suits
and layer upon layer of clinging middle management,
desperate for final nevermind.
"Speak it!" he howls to his angel.
The scream comes from his stomach,
steeped in the last of otherworld pain.
"Speak it! Let's make my losses worth the trip!"

And she
her heart fat with afternoon light,
her eyes an ancient, star-matted expanse,
finest fruit of first creation,
she stretches her wings
to a tender enfolding,
offers a memory of sun in her welcome,
pouts her jewel mouth in that
ageless, graceful, benediction,
as she says

peace
peace
peace

## Step I

Theodore Vaca
Asheville North Carolina

A man fell into a pit of fire. The wind took his ashes
to the river and he began to swim.

threshold looms
    a ghost
    procrastinates
    the case crumbles
    as the ravens fly

step another step

A magician performed a trick. He reached into a hat,
pulled out a sword, ran it through his heart and cried.

step another step

Once the walls were paper. The night wrote upon them
as they tore. The light, come morning, did not call
the day. So now, the sun still lays hidden behind
the horizon.

rock yourself
    to dream
    of angels

drink yourself
    to flush

waste yourself
    to see
    god in the mirror
        and
        christ will
        crumble
        for you

## Mother Lillith

Janet Lawless
Hamtramck Michigan

MOTHER LILLITH
How come
there are no
temples in your
honor
that I can see borne
above cityscape
rooftops
at the center of a
community
on a lonely, silent
country canal?

MOTHER LILLITH
How come?
I had to research
to find out
more
instead of entering
an edifice false front
erected
to salute a solely,
exclusively male
God?

MOTHER LILLITH
How come?
Your history
tells of a
threatening
menacing
demon
haunting their night
mares
manipulating
sexual
Evil?

MOTHER LILLITH
How come?
Instead of the
fertile
fecund
lush creator
nurturer diva

you're an
obscure,
occult,
mystical, mythical
demon-pagan
temptress
whose
Love, Power, and Might
is no less
real and ubiquitous
than his?

MOTHER LILLITH
How come?

# Love & Lust

## Cigarette Mapping

Golda Fried
Montreal Canada

I went though the day in a daze and came out the other side to find a man waiting for me there, smoking behind a dented hat, leaning against someone's car. What first amazed me about him was his thinness. He could slide in between the cracks of the street and soon I was realizing that I could do it too. We pretty much strolled right on through the night under fire-escape trees and past garbage stumps, mapping our path with cigarette breaks. Finding bits of newspaper to read like puzzle pieces. Contemplating billboard signs but not in the mood to jump off balconies into oblivion. Finding five cent pieces but no candy store was open. And as we passed through this ghost-town, I thought that this night was like any other but with a lot of harmonica thrown in. And we came to a park and sprawled out on the ground. My first reaction was to bury myself under the fallen leaves and I slid under a pile giving myself Halloween Hair. But he brushed the dry dead things off of me, one by one, and cleared out a circle on the grass in front of us. In this space, we emptied our pockets and gazed at our souvenirs. He took off his hat and placed it in the middle of the circle. Then we gave each object a toss with anticipation of what part of the heart it would strike. And when we were through with lyrics for a while, the harmonica player came through pounding out a solo, hitting all the high notes. The guy grabbed his hat and got the hell out of there before the sun came up and all the magic was gone. I had one more cigarette left to burn in this package of the unexpected and rolled it in my hand to make it last for a while. I sauntered on over to work and lit the cigarette outside the glass walls. All it took was one look at my reflection and I hitchhiked out of town.

## Love At First Sight

Jeff Meyers
Portland Oregon

it was here,
behind the hunched coven of garbage cans.

here,
in the back of the alley's throat,

that I stood,
hands on knees,
letting my stomach speak for itself
in zesty little italian sauce phrases.

and I saw her,
surveying the street for witnesses,
making her friends stand guard

as she lifted the dark paisley of her skirt,
pulled down her jockeys
and pissed in the alleyway.

she didn't see me,
as we each, in opposite squats,
broke the law with our bodies.
we were fellow conspirators,
answering only to the voice within.
the voice that said, "now, now, now!"

she pissed so hard
her eyes closed tight and
nothing moved,
not even her red curls,
as night breezes sent litter chasing around us.

"Amanda, hurry up!" whispered one of the sentries.
Did they know they were accessories to our crimes?

and she finished,
jitterbugged in place
    three
       four
wiggles to bring the skirt down straight before leaving.

Amanda. Amanda.
   I almost called out to her.

## Scarred

Megan Clark
Austin Texas

And so his woman
rode out, unleashed libido
between her legs
unclenched enamel
still left on her teeth
unrestrained passion moussed
into a knot of blonde, hidden
beneath her velvet hat

And then she burst in
slipping just a little on
the waxed wet floor
and ordered.

Trying not to be belligerent
(procrastinating drinking)
she kept a tight hold
she kept a grip
she did not peel her
flesh right off the bone
She did not run
She did not howl
She did not grasp
and hope
and grope
for sympathy in the ravine
She did not accost him
panting wild-eyed and wet

And so she was aware
painfully and finally
of the difference in their realities

And the pain was sweet and hot
and when it flooded the roof
of her mouth she swallowed
and gagged and scarred
her arms for more.

## A Woman Now

Janice Erlbaum
Brooklyn New York

this must be it
this is what you were taught to want
this met him mouth open to kiss and *this*
two iodine fingers lynch brutal
hangnails tangle crisp hairs and
pinch your lips together

you moan, you don't wince

pushed over and in your
whole clenching nails like a fist
the chafing burn to resist his
rabid quenching does not desist
in the face of your mask
you can't deny but you're not what you do
sucking to keep from drowning
dying for it or from it
a good lover to get it over get it over

just come
hurry up and    come
just come
hurry up and    come

shaking your whole body no
no notice me notice that I don't want to
do this notice that I am dry under you scraping
raping yourself with lout and lout again
slapping return carriage pounding keys
remorse code signal furied pleas
solace only with his impending release
and you continue to survive
cauterized gouges submitted inside
the surrender of his sudden naked eyes
widen your own perverse pride
cause there's glory knowing how much
you can take before you tear
and you think  you must be
a woman now  you can bear  anything

## What You Say vs. What You Mean

Carolee Klimchock
Austin Texas

When I saw you last week, you were on the way to band practice. What are you calling yourselves now, the Born Again Bombshells? And you said, "Hey how are things, I've been meaning to call you. Let's get together," as you tried to avoid looking me in the eye by pretending you were having a contact problem even though I know you don't wear contacts. I knew you actually meant, "Oh God, not you again. I don't want to have to be nice to you anymore, but I will because I want my CDs back." And yes, I do have your CDs and no, I'm not giving them back. You'll have to fight me for them. Not that I'm listening to Ugly Kid Joe or your Beach Boys box set, but not calling, not returning my calls, and forgetting to meet me for lunch that day pretty much rules out you're ever getting them back.

And when I asked you how the band was doing and you said, "Good. We're really putting our shit together, but we're not quite where I'd like to see us." I knew you meant, "Even though we've been playing in my garage for over two years, we still suck and we haven't gotten a gig yet." Because I know you and your strung-out friends and how band practice turns into a sitting around, drinking, watching *Dukes of Hazard* reruns, talking about sex and how underrated Brian Wilson is burp festival. So don't tell me I look great in this dress, because I know that porno-watching, junior high boyish, hard on, pea brain mentality of yours is really saying "I'm horny, what are you doing tonight?" So get lost little cretin boy and get those thoughts out of that minuscule pile of excrement which doubles for your brain. I guess I must have been raving mad or suffering from a fatal tumor which ate half my skull to ever have gone out with you. You scraggly, bleached hair, bloodshot eye, lipstick wearing, grungy backpack carrying, smelly Converse high tops, gross bathroom habits, saggy torn jeans, pseudo-political activist, cigarette breath slob. I know your type. Weren't you in that movie *Slacker*? You know when you used to say you just liked to improvise, bond with your guitar and play your own thing rather than limit yourself by the set constraints of the music industry? I know you really meant you can't read music. But then a lot of well known musicians were self taught, right? And after all you've been busy these last few years, what with the biannual Donny Osmond fan club newsletter you put out and that project you had to revive *The Gong Show* on the cable access channel. You've had your hands full. Oh and I forgot about the Bisexual Recovering Alcoholic Performance Artists for World Peace Club you started. Now that was a noble effort.

I guess I shouldn't be so hard on you, eh? I know you've been in therapy for quite a while and understandably you're having a difficult time dealing with the confession by your ex-exotic dancer mother that you're the illegitimate child of Ed McMahon. And my last name may not be Wopner, but I can judge by the way your voice changes that when you say, "My therapist says going clean is in the future and not to think so much about a quick road to wellness as a thorough one," you mean, "Help! Nurse Ratchet thinks I'm beyond hope and they may lock me up for good!"

But I'm not concerned abut your psychosomatic trauma, I always knew you were a fucking lunatic, but hear this—the next time I run into your sorry-ass in the Rock aisle at Tower Records in between Madonna and Mudhoney and you say, "Hey there spike tongue, I bet you've got a hot date for Friday night, who is he?" but you really mean, "I don't have plans, you want to go out?" I'm going to say, "Look, Beavis, don't you have some fetus worshipping festival to protest or a screening at the sperm bank to go to? Or can you just not stand being without those fishnet tights I borrowed from you last year? Move over, you're blocking my way. I'm looking for the new MC 900ft Jesus single. What are you here for, Barry Manilow or Liza Minnelli?" But what I'll really mean is, "Yeah, okay. What time should I pick you up?"

## Better Left Unsaid

Wendy-o Matik
Oakland California

It's all about:
    stating the obvious
    words without substance
    over-emphasized
    over-clarified
    he's terrified
    that this time,
        I might reveal too much
        express more feelings
        than you'll feel in a lifetime
        an emotional outpour
        pressing you further against
            that concrete heart of yours.

The ineffectiveness of sound
    and tone of voice
The failure of words
    to deafened ears
The illusion of friendship
that cannot exist in silence.
An accusation like a smack in the face
    but not to be misunderstood
    because it's disguised in love

But it always falls short for me
    because love is never enough.

    Your quiet, tender hands
    puncture my lungs
    filling them with lighter fluid
    while I spit up the strength
    to lie and say, "I understand"
And maybe I even start to believe you
    maybe I even start to believe myself
because silence breeds assumptions breeds falsity
      breeds blindness breeds
      the execution of language.

why speak? he retorts
It's all about:

stating the given
you should already know all this
reiteration leads to confusion
Communication is the enlightenment
    of knowing without being told.

who needs the verbal? he injects,
    it's the sanctity of this silent
    acknowledgment that should stand out
                above all.
    can't you see how talking about it
    only makes matters worse??

Obviously, I'm not who he (silently) thinks I am.
Obviously, He's not who I (outspokenly) think he is.

But we have an understanding,
silence is better
silence preserves our sacred concept of friendship
better left unsaid
    than to challenge the misfortune of our false
    intentions
better left unsaid
    that to disrupt
    the waters of reassurance
better left dead, and over,
              and buried
    than to wrestle with our fears
    of just how alone we really are
no matter what I say
no matter what you can't say.

## Kérosène

Martin-Pierre Tremblay
Montreal Canada

Tu vends des cigarettes. Au noir. Sur la rue. Tu vois longtemps le jour décliner, se déchirer entre les voitures. Trop de mouvement. Autrefois, tu prenais l'autobus pour aller à l'école. La même chanson revenait toujours dans laquelle un homme tue un ours à mains nues. Il y avait aussi Mara. Ce n'était pas tant l'odeur de sa peau qui t'excitait mais plutôt le contenu de ce sac qu'elle gardait près d'elle durant tout le trajet. Tu te souviens d'un ange bleu, de tout ce qu'il disait. C'était il y a très longtemps. Depuis, tu as croisé le chauffeur à quelques reprises. Il est maintenant chauve.

# What We Were

David Jewell
Austin Texas

we were
I could walk in and talk to you behind the counter where you work.

we were breakfast.
once.

maybe we were coffee.
we were probably coffee.

we might have been movie.
we were definitely matinee.

we were I want you
to look at some stuff I've been writing and see what you think.

I don't think we were drive around the lake to watch the sunset.
and when on a whim I thought maybe we could be
fancy candle-lit expensive french dinner

(just for fun...nothing romantic...)

you were
whoops! can't go out tonight after all due to cramps
call ya later

but you never called

then we weren't even breakfast anymore.
we were just barely run into each other tentative hug
big smile hi how ya doin'

maybe we'll be coffee again someday.

we'll probably be coffee.

## Formaldehyde

Manuel Schwab
Irvine California

When I die they'll doctor me like a red margarita in a bar,
and her insidious lips will finally swallow me like thick cooking
chocolate.

# Dancing

Matthew John Conley
Albuquerque New Mexico

She comes crawling in my window
at 2:37 in the morning
in a lacy white prom dress
and hair oily black like the sun that no one sees, lights

candles and puts sad Chopin playing waltzes on my stereo,
pulls me naked from my bed and close up against her
we dance,

she tugs at the edges of her dress
and we dance,

a dying horse lay dreaming in the corner
and we dance,

wine pours from her deepest mountain throat
and we dance,

I am hurting I am hurting her lips open the wound
and we dance,

and we dance
as the fire presses its tongue against the uppermost skin of the cavern,
our shadows dripping down and carving at her
with uncertain knives until the rock
lunges through the crowd and she says

no,
Matthew,
no,

no as she pulls her dress down across her hips,
no as one last sip of wine tastes my eyes and her and sad Chopin
go crawling through my window from whence they came, no, Matthew,
we can't,
we can't.

## Condoms

Clyde L. Richardson
Houston Texas

You can do a lot with condoms
Non-Oxynol-9
The clinics' favorite kind
You can drop them in soup in a casual way
Put one on, it's time to play
Cut off circulation
Make it swell like a doggie rod
Put one on when you masturbate, and
you'll have a meal when you ejaculate
Fill 'em with water to throw at cops
Rough riders are always tops
Stays hard forever
Gonna come never
Put Ben-Gay on them and give 'em to your friends
when they put them on their heads will spin.
You can choke someone to death with a condom
suffocate them in their sleep
Pull them off in the middle of sex
To have a naked dick come in their face
If you don't have one, and your
partner says no way, there's always
a gas station not far away

# Fly

Natalie Jacobson
Seattle Washington

I look at you
I think about
Cracking you open
Just to look inside
And see what you dream about

You hold my interest
For about a minute

I slit my eyes
Hoping my limited view of you
Will improve you
It doesn't

I close my eyes and try
To sink into safe, black space
But your face intrudes
Persistent, hovering

You scare me
For about a minute

I look out the window
And wonder how long
How long will this night be
Waves of time

They distract me
For about a minute

There's a fly crawling along the ledge
Looking for shit
It's on a mission
It has an agenda

Like you did
For about a minute

I left my shit out
It drew you to me

I've got to learn
Not to leave my shit lying around
Exposed, available
You don't need any encouragement

You crawl all over me
For about a minute

I rip off a wing
And look at you
Through a dirty, grey cellophane lens
You look the same

This holds my interest
For about a minute

I have no further use for it
I drop it on your face
You twitch and keep sleeping

The fly on the ledge
Is dancing in circles
Trying to find its balance

I offer my assistance
I rip off its other wing
Now, it's even

It stands still
Reassessing its new situation
Wingless, grounded, unfree

It starts to do a dance
A dizzy, circular dance
Looking for wings

Like I did earlier

When our conversation went nowhere
But round and round
Round the same moral bend
Like morality would take us somewhere

The fly keeps looking over its shoulder
For the wings that were just there a minute ago

And now they're not
But it can't help looking for them

Cause they were just there
A minute ago

You make a sound on the bed
It's a scratching, nasty noise
It's your hand
Crawling over the sheets
Looking for me

Cause I was just there
A minute ago

It sickens me
I want it to stop
I want to tear off your fingers
To make it stop

You and the fly crawling
keep crawling
Around and around

I have to make you both stop
Stop looking for what used to be

I crush the fly with my thumb
I'll deal with you
Later

## Charlotte

Jesse Higman
Seattle Washington

Charlotte from Mississippi. She blew down the doors of my life and after three days of turning the world to mulch on our giant riding mower, we still had the top down. This third night we sat together smoking pot and devouring each other's ideas. Our conversation was urgent and desperate like sex with a stranger in a bathroom. Our topics, words and stories collided and wove with force. We were engaged.

"Ooohh," she remembered suddenly, "I brought it." The barrage of conversation stopped and the room was silent, giving complete attention to the path of her hand entering her coat pocket. With binding anticipation and a grin, she pulled it from her coat. She looked like a school girl with a secret. She, however, was an adult with a gun.

It was a stainless steel Smith and Wesson thirty-eight with a molded black hand grip — and it was beautiful. We shared its beauty, complimenting its qualities like proud parents over a newborn. After a few precious moments, she lifted it from between us with the care of both hands. Swinging the cylinder out, she pushed the bullets onto the couch. They dropped into a pile and she reformed the gun. After exchanging a few good gun stories, I set it down to dent the couch next to her and our conversation scrambled on into the night.

We talked happy and sad, near and far, big and small. Our talk went the full spectrum and even made a few new colors after ultraviolet. I told her of my idea to make a foam bat called the Ugly Stick with which you could jokingly pound your friends and co-workers, and she told me of her dysfunctions. While discussing the source of creativity, I posed the question of dysfunction to her. I prefaced it with a theory.

"I've known a lot of fucked up people — not all of them are creative, but ALL of the creative people I've known are fucked up. It's almost like when they're young, they're blessed (or cursed) by the Dysfunction Stick. It's like being knighted, only overhand, and with an aluminum bat. You get whacked by this mighty blow at some point in your life and while you are sprinkled by pixie dust from the swing, you get a good chunk of bones broken. You drag your wreckage on, and while the magic of the dust illuminates your charisma for all to see, your injury goes unseen. Until... you come in close contact. Then people begin to see through the glow. They see how you limp or gimp or hobble. They see your twisted form. Some people are horrified by this disrobing of another, but I have come to love the sight. The damage is vital to the beauty it creates, and I look at them with equal and indivisible appreciation and awe. So... Charlotte, you seem like a very intense person. You can't sit still, you can't be quiet, you are a great writer. You seem to have a glow, what made you this way? What was your damage?"

She paused. "When I was young, I was fat. At twelve years old, I weighed 160 pounds. Kids made fun of me and I never had any friends. I never dated. I stayed at home a lot and watched a lot of movies — I have over five hundred on tape. I became bulimic because I hated myself. I could feel all of that changing me." She withdrew to recline, turning her head down.

I honored her story with a moment of silence, then tried to begin my words, "So that was your Ugly Stick.... I mean, Dysfunction Stick!"

The energy in the room went stagnant with the stink of the ill words. This moment reinforced the cliche of the needle scratching off the record. My mistake was not going to lie down unnoticed in a corner, the slip of the tongue was like striking a match in a gas-filled mobile home.

She exploded foreword, in a burst of red hair. She retaliated, "Ugly Stick, huh!? So you think I was ugly, too!"

Her arm was a blur as I heard the stiff ratchet of the thirty-eight's hammer cracking back tight. It was hard on my temple and pushed me off balance for a moment. While my next decision was instant, it was based on several things.

Growing up in the country, my friends and I all had guns. From BB guns in grade school to shotguns in high school. We all had many adventures with guns. Through our lessons we learned to respect the power of a gun and to fear the gun. For as squirrely and non-confrontational as thirteen-year-olds can be, there was always one time when we were straight. When a friend pointed a gun at you, whether by casual disregard or just screwing around, you were serious. Sobered from youth, you became mortal and cold. Pointing of a gun was not tolerated. After the barrel had been thrust aside and the throat had been grabbed and there was the swearing and chastising, there was silence. While even the threat of a barrel was never serious enough to separate kids, it sometimes kept us apart for up to ten minutes. During my life in the country, a couple of my friends had shot themselves. I had sat anxiously in the waiting room, and I had been shot at and intimidated by farmers, but I had never dealt with the psychology of an urban gunman, or gunwoman in this case. I had one more lesson to learn.

I looked into her eyes and she smiled for a moment as if joking. I had always wondered what I would do in this situation. I didn't get enraged, I didn't push the gun away, I didn't even say, "Please." I wanted to experience this. They say you never know until you're there, and there I was. I thought I could talk her gunned hand away from my head but now I had to do it to prove it to myself. My response was immediate. I drew in a deep breath and relaxed with the exhale. The marijuana, which got me into this whole mess, was now working in my favor. With succinct stream of consciousness I sincerely explained my mistake.

"Earlier in the evening I told you about my Ugly Stick idea. I was proud of my metaphor, and the fact that I was using the continuity of the Ugly Stick conversation to express the theory of the Dysfunction Stick." As I was talking I saw her focusing, listening intently. I was also desperately trying to count the bullets on the couch. *One- - two- -three- -four, one- -two- -three.*

"I think you are beautiful, you know that. I'm just a little high. Referring to your body as fat was a slip of my words not my heart."

The hammer flew like a rat trap, slapping into the chamber and with the sharp action and reaction of a croquet mallet, the barrel cracked against my temple.

"BANG!" she screamed. I sat frozen for a moment, waiting for my body to fall to the floor, leaving my soul upright and puzzled. Instead, I felt my spine leave my body like a long shit piling onto the floor.

"FUCK!" I yelled in disbelief. "You would've shot me! You would've fucking shot me!" My mind, only metaphorically blown, tried to regain my senses. I could only stutter half swear words in disbelief as I watched her rolling back into laughter on the futon. She held her stomach with both hands as she wailed. The gun hung limp, barrel down from her fingers, flopping like a warm dead animal with each heaving burst of laughter. "I can't fucking believe you would have shot me," I accused again.

She pulled herself forward from her laughter. Shaking her head to my face with a smile, she explained, "I wasn't even listening – I was just pissed."

## Poem

Jessica Alarcon
Raleigh North Carolina

I love to fight
I'll start off by smacking you
Dead in the face with reality
Kicking some soul into you
Knocking some culture into you
Hitting you with all the knowledge I have;

Why?
Because I love you
I'll help you get back on your feet
Help you heal the wounds society has placed on you
Bathe you in the cool refreshing waters of the motherland
Let you taste the fruits of our ancestors
And invite you to the Ancestral
There we will repair the confusion
Of your mind

## Scars

Maia Morgan
Chicago Illinois

At night at your house we lie under a blue electric blanket.
You ask me am I scared of electric blankets.
It's fine I say, it's warm. I like how it feels warmer in the
spots where the cat's paws press.

Our words string a necklace, bead by bead. You tell me about how once when
you were really depressed, just mad and drinking gin, how you got the idea of
cutting one hundred and fifty nicks,
little sluices in your arms, coaxed your skin to spill its messy secrets.
I like scars, run my fingers along their backs.

I say it's funny how girls do that.
Where did I get the idea to make my arms into paper dolls, rake
them into rose gardens, grow those sorrowful petals?

There was this Gothic girl who used to come in where I work,
with black hair like a curtain for black coffee and water.
So one day in winter she had plastic blood dripping down her arms. Redder
than real, harder, streaked down her jelly pastry arms in winter. The other waiter
whispered offhand, "I'm sorry you're in pain," and rolled his eyes when she
turned her back because fake blood, please. And it was running like a righteous
stream down her arms.

We must have remembered from ages back.
The devils must be made to exit their caves.
The doctor must be called,
the basin brought,
the wounds inflicted.
And we carry it on
with the kitchen knife, the bit of glass
Little Juliet, you have only lost yourself.
Quick
you pull your sleeves down over the tricks you played on your guilty skin.
Tiny orchards of sticky fruit blossom and fall from your limbs,
and that makes you high,
sends you inside down a long spiral, sliding gently
quiet
never screaming
so quiet

I can hear you.
Listen, I can hear you.

A bead slides. Click. A bead slides. Click.
Our necklace winds through the house,
bed
to kitchen
to back door, then out.
It laces up the holey sky.

## I Come to You

Kim Hunter
Detroit Michigan

out of the tangled world
where the invisible roots
of trees and volcanoes cradle our hearts
beyond the lines
of maps and culture
signpost for dreaming the past
between the secrets
of the womb and the shadow
at the end of days
there is a burning flower
plucked from the sun
rooted in the human
rooted in the need for hope

i come to you now
burned clear
with the deep need for hope
burned clear with love
love that we were fed in the womb
love that we carry as we carry the
marrow of those who brought us here
brought us here
by crossing oceans
gliding through sharks teeth
and machines the size of houses
those who were exiled in swamp
and migrated to deserts
with ancient names
they help us carry this love

a clear eyed love
awash with tears
more intimate than fingerprints
more intimate than our mingled sweat
or visions
of the inner self
shining through the full moon
this love we
proclaim before the world

as we know it
the world of
people joined by time
and dreams
and the sacred human accidents
of blood and desire
that we are bound to repeat

i come to you to say
from now on
we are a bridge to a moment
though atoms come apart we shall not
though the universe
spins toward dissolution
and clocks pretend to tell time
we are not moved by these things
 as we were moved before

there is not a name for this
paper that can bear a name
can also burn
and records disappear
and memories loose their roots
and tongues relax with death
but when every layer is floating in the wind
the unspeakable need for hope
will still have us
fused in love
as one
you are my every dream
and vision of the sun

## The Hudson Wakes You Up Each Morning

Regie Cabico
New York New York

Outside your window the sun makes a smash
against the darkest wave of water.
You could peek through the blinds
but it would be like an infant
opening his eyes to Promethian fire,
the first crackle, lava turning to stone.

A sea-breeze blows smoke in your throat
and you can't finish your sentence.
You could turn
off the clang of old fashioned alarm,
destroying the dream you and a hundred gulls share,
the glare from the Chrysler tower,
sidewalk renderings, colored-chalk
that fade with the slightest hint of rain
and the Sunday afternoon sound of pedestrians
stomping their soles on pavement.

You don't close the window.
Don't mind a chill through cotton sheets,
can't stop seasons
turning over
like rush-hour traffic.
Your parents wonder if they did all they could.
They wonder why you never pick up the phone.
The voice on the machine isn't you
even though he says he is.

The side of the bed your lover sleeps on
is where you first saw the sun rise in Oregon.
Your name means life. It is a new day.
So will its arms take you through the flames.

*In memory of River Phoenix (1970-1993)*

105

## I Love a Woman Who Eats Animals

Kevin Sampsell
Portland Oregon

I was not disappointed.
Her plate was delivered by the waiter and it was covered
by a plump, juicy T-bone steak.
I watched from across the dining room
with an emotion I've never experienced before.
It felt like religious worship.

She did not put any sauce or ketchup on it.

I ate my patty melt without actually looking at it.
My eyes were glued to her carnivorous mouth,
her blood-speckled teeth intoxicated,
a joyous frenzy of warm flesh...

Her eyes fluttered as tendons and gristle
waved freely like nailed-down snakes
in the healthy swamp of her gums
and unsympathetic tongue.
A small bone was swallowed.
A vein swayed like a pendulum
before bursting on her chin.

This was a strong woman who did not care
about the political climate of the country,
vegetables, or Morrissey.
Her primary concern was the preparation of her meat.

She reached up with a long red fingernail
and eagerly pushed a piece of burnt fat
back into her trap of jaws.
I was in a trance, in a fever.
She ate with her bare hands
like a savage.
She tore off her blouse
and scarred her chest with the bone.

"MORE MEAT!" she demanded, "MORE JUICY MEAT!"
I crawled to her feet and offered my hand.

## Lips

Tracy Lyall
Houston Texas

Big lips in the back seat of the bus
body detached, eyes swollen almost
to a smile in place of his lips.
puffy face. clam head. lobster cheeks.
snot on a half shell—seafood buffet
you're starving me within my malnourished love
body.
I'd like to see you blow my transfer sheet
between your lips
you'd want my dollar, but I'd tear it in half
to fold up the illusion of a whole.
Just as myself—only half, and half ass tactics
and halfway there to wherever nowhere is
taking us half the time.
Mr. Pudgy fudge I wanna lick ya face.
Where you headed?
You know me. You're just afraid to remember.
Mr. Hush-puppy shoes
trash-can, trash-can, no-way man.
He closes his eyes in a deep-set style
deep-set in himself
without me, wouldn't want to take me.
Wouldn't want to know that I'm a
carcass on strings of veins
led by my heart.
Heart pumps machinic — drains oil,
leaves grease stains on your driveway,
Heart grinds gears with lube of tears and spit.
I need just a small amount of spit
from you big ol' lips.
But you closed up and your eyelids
covered your lips
to smother you within yourself
and you were mute
Big lips with no purpose—
two extra lumps of body fat
two uneaten skin rolls
two moist slugs on your face
lips you couldn't use

107

lips left alone on seventy-five miles of
desert terrain in the back seat of the bus
to dehydrate – what a shame.
What a waste of lips.

## Locks and Keys

Crisa
St. Louis Missouri

I noticed her
From a distance
She was just walking down the street
Snaking her way around slower pedestrians
Stroking their legs with her sheer
Almost transparent sundress
Flowing in the breeze of her stride
With her cowry shelled locks
Striking each other
Ringing windchime resonance
And slapping her back
In beat
With the stride
Of her cascading dress

The jymbey and adumdum tell stories of her walk
Each ankle bracelet
Toe ring
Leather sandal
Step
Gracefully connected with foreign jungles of petrified soul trees
Making them crumble into the sands of her land of origin
Freeing their captives from their personal hells
And curing her of her homesickness

While the sun rained down on her
As if only on her
Setting her glistening forehead and bare shoulders aglow
Kissing her small frame from honey brown
To mahogany

I found myself breathless
Remembering my ancestral home
And my mother
As I marveled at her
Watched her absorb
And reverberate the elements power
As her prism eyes swallowed the sun and spat out rainbows
That stroked men's faces and turned their heads
Captured their souls and inspired their actions

They would give anything to be hers
Walk side by side with her
Have their names roll off her full lips
Drip from her dimpled chin
Dance through the air
Grab their hearts
And hold them gently
Like a reborn child in its mother's arms

But she walked with me
She called my name
And in that instant I loved her
Hoping that I would be the eleventh man

Just then the sky became overcast
Temperatures dropped
Head adornments disappeared
Sundress turned into an overcoat and sandals into boots
Covering the ankle bracelet
The toe ring
And her skin reverted back to honey brown
Reality settled in

Yet her eyes were just as intriguing
Her walk
Just as powerful
As she was just as stunning to me

## Another Brick in the Mall

Cheryl B.
New York New York

So there I was in Keansburg NJ, in the good old USA, in the house of someone whose ex-girlfriend's brother's mechanic used to know someone who was a roadie for Black Sabbath, which is why I was surrounded by the girls with the hair and the nails and the bad skin and the fluorescent orange bikinis attached to their seaside baked bodies perchance to meet Ozzy Osborne or more likely perchance to suck the cocks of the many local all male band members that were in attendance.

It was hard for me, the plump and dumpy Italian chick in my 'I'll see you on the dark side of the moon' t-shirt and black stretch pants, as I was more interested in the solution to my own suicidal tendencies than I was in Ozzy or Bon Jovi's guitarist Richie Sambora who happened to be sitting directly across from me.

I drank my fourth beer, Budweiser, which was handed to me by a guy the girl I worked with at Rickels Home Center told me was into fat chicks, he was a real chubby chaser. He was blond and tall and homely, he was wearing an Iron Maiden t-shirt and had a beard which in retrospect made him look like a closeted '70s leather man.

I lit my second joint of that day and took a good hit. I drove my car, slowly and smokily through the all-night Burger King drive-thru, my eyes blood stained and my head in the clouds, the Iron Maiden leatherman's head in my lap, my Lane Bryant stretch pants on the floor, Leatherboy burping incoherently as he attempted desperately to perform cunnilingus. The girl in the BK drive-thru was appalled although she probably didn't know what the word 'appalled' meant. Her frosted hairs stood on end, her blue eyeliner pooled in the corner of her eye. I felt like smearing the blue eyeliner down her fake red cheeks. Instead I drove off and lifted the leatherman's face out of my crotch by his hair, wishing he was a girl, preferably Sylvia Plath. Why couldn't Sylvia Plath have been licking my clit that night as I drove down Route 35?

I stopped and handed the boy my Whopper and told him to get out. He left. I drove off. I looked down and saw my pubes and I wondered if it's illegal to drive with your genitals exposed in NJ. I knew it was illegal to drive barefoot.

Oral sex was also not legal in NJ. I had therefore committed two crimes.

I was an oral offender. Pubic enemy number one. I spread my legs and fingered myself with my right hand as I was driving with my left, the taste of beer and french fries in my mouth.

I burp, I skid, I pass a Students Against Drunk Driving billboard. I think of Sylvia Plath and I burp again.

## Blowjob

Susan Ross
New York New York

So he says to me, "We don't have to have sex. Can you just give me a blowjob?"
"No," I say.
"Why not?" he asks.
"Because I don't want to," I reply.
"But baby, whyyyyyy don't you want toooooo?" he persists.

I don't know, I say. Maybe the sight of you begging pleading acting like a spoiled petulant six-year-old who got slapped in the face at his own birthday party is a turn-off. Maybe your hygiene sucks, sweat clings to the armpit of your ugly Gap sweater, I smelled a covert fart in the taxi and now a piece of your pretentious *insalata tricolore* is sticking like a green fungus to your front tooth second from the left. Do I have to have a reason?

"You don't have to make such a big deal about it," he says. It's not like I'm asking to have sex with you. It's *just* a *blowjob*."

Excuse me, did I miss something? Was there a whole new movement of the sexual revolution I slept through? Did oral sex lose status and become this routine thing you do at the end of the date? This Amy Vanderbilt of the bizarro world cretinous form of etiquette you now perform as easily as you once said to someone, "Hey, thanks, I had a really nice time tonight." No, a blowjob is sex just as surely as you are an aging Hair Club for Men guitar-playing wannabe with a hidden New Jersey agenda to seduce as many East Village artsy chippies as your limited mental capacity would allow you to.

"You women are all alike," he says. "Prancing around in your short tight 'here's my chocha' dress and then putting on the big *virgin* act. What am I supposed to think?"

THINK is the operative word here, you comic book cliché in cheap aftershave. I have never, ever considered fucking my way to the top. Why would I fuck my way to the bottom?

"I'm not asking to fuck you," he says. "You women, you're so uptight about your precious *pussies*. It's just your *mouth*."

Oh, really? Well, for your information, buddy, a blowjob happens to be in my opinion a very intimate form of carnal connection. More intimate than intercourse. See, stud, while you're on top of me, sweating, groaning, I can be anywhere I want.

I'm checking my polish for chips, reviewing my laundry list, making a food plan for the next day.

I'm writing a letter to my mother, planning a dinner party for Oscar night, shopping at Macy's.

I'm contemplating Clinton's health plan, prosecuting OJ Simpson, playing bad-girl bridge with Tonya Harding, Heidi Fleiss, and Amy Fisher.

I'm with another man.

I'm with another woman.

Now you see me, now you don't.

BUT when I kneel at your altar, you thrusting, me gagging, when I cough and sputter up a pubic hair that's trapped in my trachea, when you've arranged yourself pushing pelvically into my face at such an angle where even *your* member looms large in comparison to the size of my mouth, in short, when I am SUCKING your DICK, I am IN the EXPERIENCE. There *is* no escape.

And I say no.

For every time I did — when I didn't want to.

For every woman who fucked because it was easier than an argument.

For every high school girl who surrendered her cherry because 'it's not *nice* to get your boyfriend all worked up like that besides you *owe* him something for that high-profile bowling date'.

For everyone of us who opened our legs because they opened their wallets, I say NO.

I don't WANT to. We don't HAVE to. We fought our way through this maze of free love hype and other assorted miscellaneous sexual propaganda, and now we are TAKING BACK THE NIGHT!

"Oh," he says. "Well... Can I have a hand job?"

## My Country, *My Cunt*

Liz Belile
Los Angeles California

Stinks, *smells like night blooming jasmine.*
In trouble, *gets me in trouble.*
On fire, *on fire.*
Feels like a riot, *feels like a rainstorm.*
Fills the earth full of holes, *feels like a hole in the earth.*
Humiliating, *makes me proud to be woman.*
The fear of women giving birth, *making birth possible.*
Worships cock, *wants cock—sometimes.*
Bloodthirsty, *blood.*

Doesn't care if women come, *wants all women to come and
come as much as they possibly can —without jeopardizing the
fact that they may have to get out of bed once in a while.*

Warlike by nature, *warlike when necessary.*
Famine, *feast.*
Wants to put its fingers into everything,
*wants fingers. Wants freedom.*

Was a foreign home to Salvador Dali,
*is homefront for Inanna and Kali.*

Believes that it's the center of the universe,
*IS the center of the universe.*

My country, *my cunt.*

## The Ache of Loneliness

Kevin Draine
New York New York

The ache of loneliness got sick and puked all over
    the man's brand new black biker jacket.
This got the man really pissed off because he was just on his way out
to a really cool wrap party for the latest hip independent film
    to be shot on location.
Of course, he wasn't in the movie but he knew a lot of people who were.
He kicked the ache of loneliness across the livingroom floor,
wiped the puke off the jacket's sleeve and shoulder with
these thin blue paper napkins his roommate keeps buying,
and wore the new jacket anyway, saying
"Fuck it, I don't want anyone to like me anyway — fuck it."

## Homemade

John Potash
Washington DC

Served on a spat-
u-loved me for convenience.
Broken in, I'm worn out
of your white plaster caste system c-c-cocoon.
I knocked on
it
was hollow
wouldn't open
and there I was
tupper wary and weary
carelessly
saran-wrapped, bad-rapped
a rap without rhymes
reasoned in
seasoning
day in day out
t'taste good to them.
EAT ME
and skin'll hang
from the roof of your mouth
'cause I'm microwaved larvae.
Burning out of your container
I won't hold my food down
or adjust my temp-
or-meant anything I wouldn't
rraanntt.

## Love is a Hardass Thing

Steve Abee
Los Angeles California

Love is a hardass thing,
working like a mountain works its stones
back to the sea   that was its first breeze and
will always be,   is beautiful muscles spent in
the deepest NO WORDed ocean,
is harder than the softest wind is to answer with sure lips
and right moves, and love is all you got to give it all,
cause love is everything alive on the streets, broken in your head
dead in your front yard, bound to address numbers of houses
you never ever see
Love is everything, a needle wedded to your veins, never turn from it,
never try to run, for then it's a ghost and a demon, a devil
calling you down to sleep and just dream, cause then it's
an Angel walking away on a cat's night back, the moon peeking
bloodshot eyes over the tears it's laid in the waves,
love is the blind beautiful bed that sees no one, that holds many graves,
that shakes every birth, that calls you home, sweet swaying ride,
that is our lips, our bones, melted and held tight,
held with the voice in bloodful darkest spot of the womb,
Oh Love is the rain time, is the slow time, the low steam
that pulls our hands close to the stone of the wind,
holding each finger for the million years we've known
and forgotten each other,
the million years it will take
till we find us again,
the million years that we will
never be lost
Oh love is no falling thing, not like a building or an Empire,
not like dreams, it works, it works and not with clocks
or gears or hours or days, and it will not pay, and there are no schedules
it works, it works in bone and blood, in brains and eyes
in mouths and veins, in fingers across your stomach, in bellies
singing across the roofs,   digging down to the ground,
in hearts running through your lips, in the quiet
when the cars sleep       and the trees      nod the way,
Oh Love, it is a hardass thing, it is a just thing,
just going down, just coming round         breaking
with the rising sun          splintering jewels and oceans
to be just        your eyes          down the street

## What It's Like That You Are To Me

Jonathan Goldstein
Montreal Canada

It's a mama's boy meal — the soul-food music of a song of triumph in a blue, airplane-model room of the house-food of the soul. It's a cousin George basement dance of Pepperidge Farm cake of the cheeze curds of the brain in a red plastic booth of the midnite heartache of crying naked in a restaurant bathroom of the mind. It's a two-for-one Pepperoni pizza of the lunch-mother of the schoolyard of the soul. A heart attack black leotard of the Double Deuce booth of the french toast of the mind — an Arkanoid sauce of the soul. It's a gravy-train hospital cafeteria-style routine of the Sloppy-Joe of the mind — a Ponderosa birthday steak of the soul's colon problem. A diarrheal hot hamburger of lost love — the buffalo winged angel of the soul's red eye — a blue cheese dip of Heavenly love. It's a 15% tip of the rapier thrust of the pogo-stick of the mind — an aged French Bravo Burger waitress of the midnite suicide fantasy hunger for house-food eggrolls. It's a green Mister Freeze of the dead childhood schoolyard crazy lady in a mumbling hunchback shawl of a two-for-one lard poisoning. It's a chopped liver entree icecream ball on the grade five Judy Blume book report — a side order of shit blintzes on the next door neighbor's panties of the mind. It's a muddy mustard globule in a brown old man hat in the 24-hour sauna bath of the soul. It's a baby blue Speedo bathing suit of the homemade grape Popsicles in the downstairs freezer of the soul's mental breakdown. It's a Sunday night Gus the Wonder Mule Walt Disney special of the can't-sleep-got-the-squirts—neighborhood-bully-stole-my-father's-car of the mind. It's an all you can eat soul-food buffet of a naked spreadeagled ballet of a Rocket Robin Hood deep sea kiss.

## The Life Of A Ham Sandwich

Jeff Cochran
Phoenix Arizona

The only job Kurt was considered capable of handling was driving an automobile, full-time, in traffic. He was hired by Pap to deliver food to people. Pap's Pizza Place was dirty and losing money. The health inspector recently scored them a 62 out of a possible 100 points concerning cleanliness. Their pitfalls were listed in the Sunday paper. Everything from mouse shit to pigeon piss. They lost the most points for wedging the unfolded pizza boxes between the wall and the toilet in the employees' bathroom. The health inspector claimed that splattered piss can spread disease. This meant the workers had to find a new place to put their cigarettes when they shit.

Pap had a daughter. Her name was Andrea. Andrea was young and beautiful but she was far from pleasant. She had worked in the restaurant for many years and she was probably diseased as well. Kurt was secretly in love with Andrea. Andrea thought Kurt's name was Kent. She never really looked at him because, after all, she said, "He's an idiot and I'm not." Kurt watched her and he knew her work schedule. He dressed special on the days she would be there.

One day, a ham sandwich rolled out of the timed oven and Kurt set it on the prep counter so as he could wrap and deliver it. Andrea was pissing in the diseased toilet on the other side of the flimsy kitchen wall. Kurt could hear her water tinkling into the porcelain bowl. It was music. The sound suddenly stopped and there was two seconds of silence. Kurt could hear Andrea spin off several squares of toilet paper. Silence. Kurt stood with his eyes open and imagined her right hand dabbing the soft skin between her legs. He heard her work her tight jeans back up to her tiny waist and he heard her zipper roar up. The toilet flushed and the door flung open and there Kurt stood, wanting to smell her unwashed hand.

"What's the matter?" Andrea asked.

"I wasn't sure if this sandwich was done yet," Kurt replied.

Andrea frowned and stepped up to the prep table next to Kurt. The ham sandwich lay there ridiculously. Andrea lifted the corner of the bread and she plunged her right index finger deep into the center of the sandwich. "It's warm," she said. Then, without ever looking at Kurt, she pulled her finger from the sandwich and she placed it deep within her mouth. Her lips closed delicately around her second knuckle and she pulled it slowly from between her teeth, cleansing her finger of the warm sandwich juice.

Kurt's dick began to fill with hot blood. He quickly wrapped the sandwich with paper, dropped the sandwich in a bag along with a pickle spear and he bolted out the door and into his car. Kurt joined the traffic in a crazy motion. He steered the car with his knees as he dumped the sandwich into his lap allowing the pickle spear to drop to the floor. He frantically unwrapped the ham sandwich and peeled apart the bread. He sniffed the meat like a dog sniffs a well-traveled tree. He wanted to smell something besides ham. At the first stop light he undid his pants and allowed his swollen dick to breathe. He held the warm ham sandwich in his right hand, while his mind replayed the scene of Andrea licking her finger. He wrapped the soft, warm sandwich around his raging hard-on and he held it there for exactly 37 seconds. His mind was like a microwave. A bell went off in his head and he carefully returned the ham sandwich to the wrapper and he placed the sandwich back in its brown paper bag and he drove to the proper address. He surrendered the sandwich and he accepted a generous tip.

Back at Pap's place the phone rang and Andrea answered. It was the recipient of the ham sandwich. He called to complain. It seemed as though he did not receive his pickle spear and when it was all said and done and when the pickle spear was dead and gone and when the phone was taken off the hook and the oven set to cool, no one knew anything more than they had ever known before and the world took another spin and the people took another turn and Kurt took another step toward Andrea.

## Love Song in Case of Goodbye

Evert Eden
New York New York

I loved you because you were fiction cross-dressed as fact
your lips a sweet saga from Homer
    your silence a speech from Jane Austen
    your sex a lake sucked dry by Sappho
    your soul bluer than the bluer-than-blue blued-out blue blue
                with which Matisse fought the sky

          but you
          you saw the undertow
          a shape of many teeth, shark-silent
the fin, the jaws
a severed heart bobbing
orphaned on the ocean of a dream

all I ever wanted was to be the tongue
that learned the whisper of your body like a language
the hand that played you up and down like scales
the eye that saw a flush run
like a herd of buffalo over your chest into your eyes

listen
If we should split like two wings that break a bird
because they flap in opposite directions
remember the hour of greendumb delight
before a black cloud dropped a pot of spleen on us
let those broken wings fly to the east and the west
and tell of the doing we done did—
        how we watered the sun with sex
        yanked the moon to our bed headfirst
        raised a love that milked the stars
        and sugared the salt of the earth

## Song in the Key of Nicole

DJ Renegade
Washington DC

She was Miss sweet potato brown,
a steamy cocoa statuette with
  caramel-colored eyes
      that were always in search of something.
And with pepper tongue twirling,
  she set whole rooms whirling,
      her dark beauty swirling,
so devilishly dervish
  and needlessly nervous
      though wordlessly,
      wordlessly weird.
And after having seen her
  men would stumble into drugstores and
      desperately unwrap all the Hersheys bars
      in search of similar brown sweetness,
but she refused all flowers,
  would hold no hands,
      and slept in heavy sweaters as though
      frantically afraid of the cold.
And I think it was over herbal tea
  that I noticed in the shadows of her smile,
that she'd slept in passion's alley
  and searched through all the cans,
but found it left her hollow
  with strangely smelling hands,
and still not finding....

## Darling, I'm All Yours

Marlys West
Austin Texas

The new trick
is to get to know them
show them
how lovely you are
show them
all your charming
ways

Trickle in
bit by bit
all of the spicy
details
of your life
your broken leg
your
predilections
for pills
and razor blades

by the time
you're finished
we're certain
he'll be mesmerized
amazed at
your ingenuity
dumbfounded
by the prospect of
this hard woman
before him
the same girl
who shakes
at night
charming in her
own strange ways

Darling I have
something
to tell you

I don't know
how I made it
this far
far enough to reach
your arms
it's been a
long deranged
trip and I've only
a few hang ups
only
a few doctors
and really
the prescriptions
aren't much
to talk about

Where did you say
you wanted to take
me this evening?

## Upstairs

Laura E.J. Moran
Asheville North Carolina

The youngest ones borrow
change from their fathers,
drive slow past neon saxophones
and point out
              their older brothers
lingering with smoke on the street.

Stopping, they
              and whistle
at silk legs because it is all
they can do.

One by one
the oldest disappear
upstairs to beat desperation
into Venus' gnarled face.
                  She
has no teeth,
              and they
are pleased when she unzips
flies with her lips.

## The Body Politic

Richard Loranger
San Francisco California

Rumble rumble in the jumble
neurons burn & thoughttrains tumble
through the mind & out the hole
the world has punctured in your soul
& if you fear you're running out
feel free to clear yourself from doubt
& reproduce your darling strains
from any of your thousand brains
& though it's true you're one in a million
you're just as well a million in one
& I will strive to make you see
that all of you are equally
yourself & if you truly feel
you are an individual
it's true but only by concession
of all your selves in joint congression
as throngs of microscopic men
conjoin to form a common ken
as laws of any governed nation
build generation on generation
until they reach an evolution
through rotation or revolution
your self is just a nicety
to pacify society
a ledger where you keep defined
the current status of your mind
your mind to take the other hand
is the machine by which you stand
to organize your countless factions
into a man of thoughtful actions
& though it's good to seek perfection
you should unveil with some reflection
that notions of utopia
are functions of myopia
because of course the world's a churning
vat of minds that's always burning
burrows in your psychic force
but that's the joy of intercourse

for just as you're indeed a body
politic you in reverie
interchange your population
with every other body nation
in all complexities of trade
by which your changing self is made
 & in this lies a quiet key
to the supposed mystery
of the integrity of mind
it's an imaginary line
we draw a mental hocus-pocus
the flesh is really just a focus.

# Societal Squalor & Politics

## The Complete Failure of Everything

Jose Padua
Washington DC

At the carnival sideshow
the veteran sword swallower has bloodied his throat.
The snake charmer has been attacked,
his cobras, rattlers, boas
have stung, bitten, and squeezed him to death.
In the tunnel of love the teenage couple
keep their hands at their sides
and look straight ahead,
waiting anxiously for the ride to end.
Out on the rollercoaster people are yawning
while on the merry-go-round children
are screaming in terror.
In the suburbs a man has decided
not to build a deck on the back
of his new house.
His neighbors are at the mall
attending the grand opening
of a multiplex porno theater.
Back in town the crack dealers
and junkie hookers
are giving it away.
The Jehovah's Witnesses are wandering around
drunk, cigarettes dangling from their mouths
as they mumble, "Jesus, I just don't know."
In the universities the professors
have taken over the libraries.
They're tearing up the pages
of every book on every shelf
on every subject.
In the nightclub the stripper
with the 72-inch bust is keeping her top on
while the flat-chested women rip open their blouses
and shout, "Va Va Voom,"
to the delight
of the already frenzied crowd.
The billionaire is sitting on a park bench
perusing the want ads
while the panhandler orders dinner
at a fancy French restaurant

for fifty of his closest friends.
Over in the third world
the mercenary is helping to build a hospital
while the Christian missionaries
have just raped and pillaged
in a small town of peasants.
There is snow in the desert
and flowers in the arctic,
wild music in the asylums
and silence in the dance halls,
charity in the casinos
and greed at the Salvation Army,
orgies in the convents
and prayers in the whorehouses.

And what we are witnessing
is the complete failure of everything.
The failure of the rich and the poor.
The failure of the ecstatic and the tortured.
The failure of the loud and the peaceful.
The failure of love and hate,
the beautiful and the ugly,
the good and the bad,
the daring and the timid.

It's the failure of the holy to stay holy
and the sinners to keep sinning,
the failure of the rich to stay rich
and the poor to stay poor,
the failure of those who love
and those who hate,
everything failing,
inevitably falling into its opposite,
into its enemy, into its nightmare,
into the end
where the big bang,
having reached its limit,
reverses itself,
with everything you know
falling apart,
here, in the carnival
where the last great act
is to take something,
and through a swift sleight of hand
turn it into nothing

as the bright lights dim
and the merry-go-round
grinds slowly
to a complete
and silent
stop.

# STITUTION

## Rituals

Marci Blackman
San Francisco California

*"A ritual is a behavior pattern that has lost its function." —Dan Langton*

an old man lives on the curb in front of the Wells Fargo (16th & Mission)
every once in a while he asks himself how he's doing
just to see if he's still alive

"How ya doin, Max?" he asks.
"Max is stayin alive."

guess he doesn't feel it
when the hawk that lands with the moon each night
starts nibbling on his toes

guess he doesn't really notice
when the mites and ticks
pitch their tents in the caverns of his ears
crawl through his hair looking for food

like the morning dump
grinding coffee
the second cigarette after the second cup
it's his ritual

*How ya doin, Max?*
*Max is stayin alive.*

when the brothers thought it would be cool
to hold him down one night
burn camel holes into his chest
wondering if he ran water or blood?
he didn't feel it

when he wakes each morning to a sun
hot enough to fry the grease on his skin
forcing him to scratch til dark
before it peels off
doesn't notice

it's the glass of wine before dinner
choosing between stir fry & fettuccine
gas after refried beans
*How ya doin, Max?*

shaking the dice before you shoot 'em
making the list before buying the groceries
preparing the lie to tell the cops

folding the clothes after the wash
emptying shells from chambers
after last shots
stepping on cracks in the concrete
sharpening knives from the kitchen drawer
bleeding (if you're lucky)
the 28th day of every cycle
*How ya doin, Max?*

heard he got beat up real bad the other night
matrix patrol
took a couple of billy clubs to his temples
made the cigarette holes look like needle marks
the needle marks melted back into his veins

of course, they denied it
claimed all they did was
relieve his cart
of the junk
he'd spent the last ten years collecting

said he stole it
stole all those broken bottles
said it was against the law
*How ya doin, Max?*

still see him every now and again
on my way home from work
everyday
he's wearing a different outfit

yesterday
it was a pink taffeta bra
over a dingy white T-shirt

the day before
orange sweatpants w/shit stains in the seat
& a gray sweatshirt
w/red & white letters spelling 49ers down each arm

something inside me wants to reach out and hold him
rock him back and forth
(a baby in my arms)

tell him:
*Max, everything's gonna be alright, man*
even if it does mean holding my nose
even if it is a lie

instead, i just keep walking
ask him how he's doing as i pass
he doesn't miss a beat
as if he had asked the question himself, he says:

"Max is stayin alive."

## Single Family Dumpster
A true story of Hollywood

Garland L. Thompson, Jr.
Austin Texas

She lived in a single family dumpster,
this flower of the earth,
a young babe in arms to the millennia
only fourteen years of age
human age body
yet already older than the hills
that only came around
a few thousand years ago.

Hollywood found her
pushing a shopping cart
and keeping her younger brother
from dashing across
Sunset and Highland
against the light.

She knew if he did
he would surely get hit
by a film truck on its way to location
or some guy in a 2802
and she couldn't let that happen
because she lived in a single family dumpster
the kind of place that was all the rage
among the nouveau homeless not only
congregating in Hollywood and downtown L.A.
but in Brentwood, Westwood
ritzy West L.A. and Culver City
where Mexicans hung around the movie lots
hoping to get a job painting sets or
painting something.

She was privileged because she had this
little chunk of space made of metal
resting on little metal wheels,
a sort of motorhome without a motor
that the Mafia-controlled garbage trucks
came to pick up and empty
every Thursday.

And this single family dumpster
that she rented
from no one for no money
served her well,
after all,
sleeping in it was better
than banging your head against the curb
as you passed out from the exhaustion
of always watching your ass,
always trying to grow a pair of eyes
in the back of your head
so you don't have to turn around
to know someone was creeping up on you.

She knew all this
and thanked god
for the decency it had
to provide her with a
single family dumpster,
the latest model with two spare lids,
one for each half of it,
so she could open them like
the kitchen door
at your grandparents' house in the country,
the one where you can open
just the top half or
just the bottom half
depending on what mood you're in.

Two separate lids
Two separate fathers
one for her and one for her brother,
both angry drunks who shot their wad and split,
the latter was also a crackhead who beat her
and her mother in drug-induced rage,
and eventually got hit
by a Range Rover
as he tried to cross
Sunset and Highland
against the light,
too fucked up to tell anyway.

## O Say Can You See

Ray McNiece
Willoughby Ohio

O say can you see
this country free
of bigotry, hostility, and incivility
from sea to shining tee-vee?

The tribes are picking up sides
from Bosnia to Beirut to Belfast to L.A.
and there's nowhere left to hide
for the children of the dream
walking hand in hand
down the black and white wound
running across this land.

What's wrong with this picture?
Can you find the human
being beaten on this screen?
Being beaten on this screen?
He deserved it. Payback happens.
What goes around, comes around
said the eye for an eye blind men.
But the rioting is on the wall.
Mr. President, you have a call
on the white courtesy phone.

"It's the BLANKS fault. The BLANKS
started it. You know how they are."
"They don't really belong here."
We sell ourselves on talk-shows
like bugs shaken in a jar.
And the finger of blame points around
in an angry trigger circle.
We're all living in the same 'hood,
buying into Babylonian hype.
Mad Ave. went to bed with Holly Would
and made a little family of stereotypes.

Hey red, white, blue-black,
sun and green can you see
somebody looks just like me,

somebody looks just like me
peering out from the leaves
of your family tree
rooted in mother Africa?
We are the children of the dream
who wandered our separate ways
a long time gone, gathered together
here again today. Remember?
Can we call ourselves sisters? Brothers?
What color was the hand
raised against Abel
after it fell? How will we ever
wipe the slate clean
when the powers that be
sell us whitewash cracker,
sell us spraypaint nigger,
so we can paint ourselves
in our own little corners,
the mirror of our monsters?
Can you see the eyes
of a mother, father, sister and brother
behind the masks of your worst nightmares?

O say can you see
through the lies that we are not us?
That we are always us — versus?
And where is Justice, or is it Just Us?

We are the children of the dream
wandering the desert
of America through the smoke
from the fire next time come,
walking hand in hand
down the black and white wound
running across this land
healed over with each step
together — O say can you see
the person walking next to you?

## If We Only Knew

Abiodun Oyewole
New York New York

If we only knew what we could do
We'd stop fussin and fightin and feelin blue
If we only knew that we have juice
Cause of an African connection
That we can't cut loose
If the light was in our minds
We wouldn't dis ourselves so much all the time
We'd stop and realize without disguise
We got the power to change what's before our eyes
Where there is poverty and misery
We'd bring hope, joy, love and security
There wouldn't be no need to lock your doors at night
No one lives in the dark
Cause everyone sees the light
If we only knew just how bad we are
We'd make the sun disappear
Cause we're the brightest star
If we could feel the strength
And help those who are weak
And be steppin to the rhythm like Malcolm speaks
So you thought you were a chicken
And your butt was made for kickin
You been running around
With your head hanging down
Looking for chicken feed
In this city of greed
Open up your eyes
Don't you know you can fly
Like an eagle to the sky much higher than high
Where you don't need no crack, smack or patty wack
And all the bones from that dog
You can give them right back
If we only knew what we could do
We'd stop fussin and fightin and feeling blue
Just like we cut our hair in an African style
We show rich, royal treasure every time we smile
Now sometime ago we just didn't know
That we had the power to make the whole thing go
Motivator, educator we're a power generator

We need to own the joint
Instead of working as a waiter
If we only knew how strong our will
No matter what's been done
Our soul can't be killed
Like the sun and the moon and all the stars above
It's a natural thing for us to share our love
We're a healing force in the world of pain
Trying to use common sense where life is insane
If we could recognize just who we be
We'd take control of our lives and live with dignity

## Dead Presidents

Invisible Man
San Francisco California

Find a penny, pick it up,
and all day long...

What was Lincoln really thinkin' of the life in me
Same thing they were thinkin' when they put him on a penny
A bunch of pennies in a fist for representing us
For real estate I'd buy a piece of photocopied dust
I'd make a little flag for my dust to represent
Cause brothers claiming Fillmore don't own shit in it

I wanted Armaggedon, they gave me Armaghetto
and sweat me like a sweater during summers of Soweto
So walking on the gravel wondering and mighty will
Why those who clutch the pennies never clutch the dollar bills
They hold the deeds of slaveries and riches that they've bled
So these are motherfuckin' evil spirits in my pockets

My conscience of a fueling fire for collecting them
It seems that I'm addicted to the heads of dead white men
Cause everything we do has been rewarded with a grim
picture of the ancestors of those who did mine in
And if that isn't bad then every Sunday on a cross
They take me to another one and tell me that he's God

And that's why now you see us sittin' idol worshippin'
Our mental turned a circus left abandoned
      Abandoned
Abandoned were our temples
books of wisdom and since then
You've got my people prayin' to some dead white men

Now mystery's secrets are deep but peep this —
Take another couple hundred years to see this —
You'll find Jesus, cross all glittered up,
Holding a guitar and lookin' like Elvis,
Tellin' you he's from outer space or Texas
Pennsylvania Connecticut Memphis
That's not Jesus, no, it's St. Nick
Michelangelo's cousin on a crucifix

## Vet

Regina McCullough
Pittsburgh Pennsylvania

I hated rice
In grade school when they served it
The others ate it with milk and sugar
While I stood chanting pig food, pig food

My father hated rice
He said it came from fields called paddies
When old ladies pissed
And children with dirty feet worked

My father survived two tours of Vietnam
He was an expert at rice growers
And human assassination
He has medals to prove the latter

He had seen the world
And eaten from gold cans
At home even, safe and dry,
He would take cover

Don't smack your lips
Don't eat with your hands
Don't let her nose run
Eddie wha ba teige

When my father ran a fever mom would plead, lie still
He would beg for his mess kit
Promise to stay in the tree
And ask if she would check for snakes

My father wasn't Peace Corps
He wasn't G.I. saviour
My father was a sharpshooter
He was an eighteen-year-old kid

From West End and his first trip
Out of the square block
Was to be trained to snipe targets
Pop the heads off kids carrying grenades

My father wasn't peace
He wasn't love
He never Sat In anywhere
He was good son of a WWII Dad

Kill or be killed
My father was true G.I. sprayed orange
Carrying the souls of all those lost to him

## Johnny

Sarge Lintecum
Phoenix Arizona

My friend Johnny
He got sick, you know
He got so bad
He couldn't walk or talk

He just laid there shakin' and sweatin'
Sweatin' and shakin'
And when he'd open his eyes
And look at me

I could hear a scream for help
As loud as if he had a voice
But there ain't no help
That's about as rare as hope on the streets

We all told him
Not to keep drinkin' that hair tonic
It'll kill ya, Johnny
But he wouldn't listen

When he couldn't panhandle
Enough for a real bottle
That's just what he's do
He'd say, "Dyin' ain't as bad as bein' out"

So then he up and died on me
There was five of us
A-sittin' around Johnny
Passin' a bottle

When we heard this breath come out of him
That everybody knew was his last
You never seen homeless people
Disappear so fast

A politician's dream come true
No last words, no goodbyes, nothin'
I lost guys in Nam, but damn,
We cared then

I quit askin' folks for money
For a long time after that
I just collected cans
'Cause nobody cares about the homeless

Nobody cared about Johnny
And nobody'll care when I die
It's kinda like we're doin' society
A big favor anyways, dyin' that is

If the average life of a homeless person
Is four or five years
Johnny said he read that somewheres
Then I guess I've overstayed my welcome

Folks seem to just want us gone
You know it wouldn't take long at all
To get rid of us homeless people
Just four or five years

## Home Is Where The Apartheid Is

Kedrick James
Vancouver British Columbia

I cannot write another poem about traveling
I cannot write another poem about everything
being so different, so new, it fattens up
the industry of forgetting.
I will not celebrate another culture
to the impoverishment of my own.
I will stay at home
there is work to be done at home
I can no longer drug myself on movement
and the perpetual recreation
of my past. I cannot dream up
another caricature of me
recall the child's transient reality
or swill adventures romance
saccharine sweet like Brazilian coffee
or worse, Earl Grey tea.

Home will not live out my privilege
Home will not live out your lifestyle
My maw will vomit up the hemorrhage of exotica
my paws will claw at the fawning traders with their hordes
of pricey rice paper prints and Guatemalan knapsacks
Egyptian papyrus paintings or South Asian batiks.
With the zeal of a recently reformed smoker
I will come at them
with the sweatshops gargoyled brows I will come at them
I will come at them with hopes
for my home, reasons not to shoot
uproot the political community
rout a state with a mandate against humanity
and the betterment
of minority and poverty.
We cannot hope to outlive privilege
God cannot hope to outlive privilege!
For Christ's Sake—
we cannot condemn South Africa's apartheid
and condone our own.
We cannot continue to write poems
about traveling

with the Klan cruising our home.
WE CANNOT CONTINUE TO ACCEPT MOCK EQUALITY
with a ticket to the next rip-off
"can you say Hate-E"
burning holes in your back pocket.

## Mrs. King and I

Marika
New York New York

I met you, Mrs. Coretta Scott King. We were on a plane headed to New York, Kennedy. Somehow I got my Grandfather and me into the very first seats of First Class and I sat next to you (seat 3E), for one hour and a half. I wondered whose bags were in my seat, and when you came out of the lavatory I helped you by placing them in the overhead and you wondered, "Who is this nice lady?" and I wondered, "Who is this lady who smells so nice?"

When we were seated, the coach travelers herded past us and greeted you like a line of guests to royalty. I still didn't know who you were for sure... I just thought you knew a lot of people.

An Indian Hindu woman had a baby stroller and I told her she could put it up in the First Class closet, thinking that would help her out best, and the waitress in the sky told the Hindu lady that those closets were for her "first class coats only."

I turned to you, Mrs. King, and said, "I just believe in equality for everyone, ya know? Despite the class thing," and you nodded and smiled. I introduced myself, "Hi, I'm Marika," and you shook my hand and said, "Hello, I'm Mrs. King... Mrs. Coretta Scott King. It's a pleasure to meet you." You were on your way to South Africa to greet Nelson Mandela.

## Haunting Flavors

David 'Dirt' LaSpaluto
Phoenix Arizona

I get outta my car in that Smitty's parking lot, I think I'm goin' in to get some gum & I see this homeless guy — well, I don't *know* he's homeless, but he's got that sorta lived-in look, like he forgot to come in outta the rain one time too many, only it's always sunny here, so with a sunny grin he asks, "I, uh — a quarter, man, just a quarter." Only I don't got a quarter — what do I look like, a change machine?

So I go in, I get my gum. Now I got a quarter but I figure I'll give him a dime, a nickel, so I go back to the lot & he's not there. Oh well. Go to my car & there he is. "Hi there," I say & then I realize, he's in my car, sitting in the passenger seat. "Hey, what're you doing in my car, man?"

He says, "You got a quarter?"

I give him a nickel & say, "Get outta my car."

He says, "It's not your car. You can't own the steel outta the earth, you can't take the rubber outta the rubber trees, you can't take the oil & say it's yours."

I say, "No, I can. Look, here's my registration. Now get out."

So he says, "Signs, signs, everywhere the signs," & he starts singin' that song that I always sing when I feel rebellious, feel like growin' my hair real long & trespassin'.

So I say, "All right, man, let's go, you don't sing well but you try." So I start driving, going everywhere with him & he comes along to my classes, work, home, really embarrasses me, too, keeps askin' my friends for quarters, my friends start makin' funna me: "Davey had a little homeless guy, & everywhere that Davey went," well you get the point. So I tell him, "This has got to stop," but he keeps gettin' into my car. I've given him all my quarters, always singin' that song, "Signs, Signs, everywhere the signs, blockin' up the scenery, breakin' up my mind, do this, don't do that, can't you read the signs." I tell him, "Cut that out."

Then we get real goofy & go on job interviews together with our hair up under our hats & gettin' the job, then comin' back with our hair down — we fooled some people! But then, & this is the clincher, he comes to poetry readings with me & worst of all he judges all my poems, gives me really bad scores too, & I say, "You can't do that, that's my soul, my art, this means something to me," & he

says, "No man, I can, see, here's the score," & then he starts scorin' me everywhere:
on dates, eatin' dinner, my drivin', my hair — I get to a poetry reading & he's still
doin' it & we yell at each other, "Do this, don't do that, can't you read," & the
argument heats til all across the Valley you can hear screamin', "Signs! Signs!
Everywhere     the     signs!"     &     at     the     climax     of     the     song     he
spontaneouslycombustsBOOM!

leaving behind only the lonely yapping of coyotes,
the bitter haunting taste of tequila,
a train whistle in a lonely New England darkness,

& I get in my car & drive
home
alone
in the long, songless
desert
night.

## Rez Time

Jules Dinehdeal
Phoenix Arizona

The clothesline rattled and whipped the acid-washed jeans high into the air
The rainbow of silks and velveteens quickly dried
    under the solemn eye of the sun
The pounding drumbeat of the basketball against the hardened red-clay court
Oft' times used as the Rez residential street
Half times mused in MVP feats
Now resonates between mobile homes and immobile hogans

Cousins of cousins
Navajo nephews of early teens
With Hopi tears of joy from neighboring Moenkopi
Belabor Tuba City folk into resolute sadness for the Before Times

The Before Times
Before government housing
Before inter-tribal discrimination
Before Navajo-Hopi land disputes
Before commodities
Before Hanta Virus
Before AIDS

These brothers grew up together side by side
Without loss of pride
Without loss of religious heirlooms and legends cursed and crushed
Between the coral-canyon skies and the Red Earth

The Red Earth
The land in Rez Time
The hand of Rez signs in unspoken words
Tokens of signed language not written
Only passed on from
Father to son
Son to son
Daughter to daughter
Mothers of the Clan
Mothers of the span between the legends
Between the tribes
She becomes the scribe of
Tradition found and lost
Volition lost then found

revival

Wake up brothers
Wake up sisters
Wake up distant Navajo cousins, Hopi cousins
Breathe in new life into the dying cultures
Breathe in new hope into the crying future of Rez Time

## Dispose of the Monster

Angelo Moore
Los Angeles California

The Monster of Miscommunication is
Meddling with our Minds.
Mastering up Malay in
your Memory
And Mumbling your Means
of Communication.

I think i'm turning Japanese, and I
don't know no english. it seems like now
It's Breakin & Desentegratin' & Metamortifacatin'
and discomboobyulatin the line of communication
rhyme to my Brothahs.
How will my brothahs get it right
if we don't communicate?

Searing my cerebrum with frequencies
of.....Misconception!
Did you ever hear two people sit
and......Miscommunicate?

It blow my mind into a new dimension
.....they were sparrin
with word gloves.

HE SAID "YES", SHE SAID, "YES I
KNOW", HE SAID, "NO THAT'S NOT
WHAT I MEAN". SHE SAID, "YOU
DO MEAN YES DON'T YOU?"
HE SAID, "NO I DON'T MEAN
YES I KNOW" HE SAID, "YES, I
KNOW WHAT YES MEANS."
SHE SAYS, "ARE YOU TRYING TO TELL
ME I DON'T KNOW WHAT YES
MEANS" HE SAID "YES MAYBE NOT."

At that very moment these two people
had turned into a Frothing Menstruating
alphabet Leaking Miscommunicating, Communication
Seekin Monsterish Phenominal
BULLSHIT!
At large
And at a Reality near you.

## Skinhead

Patricia Smith
Medford Massachusetts

They call me "skinhead." And I got my own beauty.
It is knife-scrawled across by back in sore, jagged letters.
It's in the way my eyes snap away from the obvious.
I sit in my dim matchbox,
on the edge of a bed tousled with my ragged smell,
slide razors across my head,
count how many ways I can bring blood
closer to the surface of my skin.
These are the duties of the righteous,
the ways of the anointed.

The face that moves in my mirror is huge and pockmarked,
apple-cheeked, scraped pink and brilliant.
I am filled with my own spit.
Two years ago, a machine that slices leather
sucked in my hand and held it,
whacking off three fingers at the root.
I didn't feel nothing until I looked down
and saw them on the floor next to my boot heel,
and I ain't worked since then.

I sit here, and watch niggers take over my TV set,
walking like kings and queens up and down the sidewalks
in my head, walkin' like their fat black mamas named them freedom.
My shoulders tell me that ain't right.
So I move out into the sun,
where my beauty makes them lower their heads,
or into the night
with a lead pipe up my sleeve, a razor in my boot.
I was born to make things right.

It's easy now to bend my big body into shadows,
to move where there was nothing into the stark circle
of a streetlight, the pipe raised up high over my head.
It's a kick to watch their eyes get big,
round and gleaming like cartoon jungle boys,
just in that second they know the pipe's gonna come down.
And I got this thing I like to say—hey, listen to this—
I like to say, Hey nigger! Abe Lincoln's been dead a long time.

I get hard listening to their skin burst.
I was born to make things right.

Then this reporter comes around, seems I was a little sloppy
kicking some fag's ass and he opens up his hole
and screams about it. So this reporter finds me at home in bed,
the TV flashes lickin' my face clean. Same ol' shit.
Ain't got no job, the coloreds and spics got 'em.
Why ain't I workin? Look at my hand, asshole.
No, I'm not part of no organized group,
I'm just a white boy who loves his race,
fightin' for a pure country. Sometimes it's just me,
sometimes three, sometimes 30.
AIDS will take care of the faggots, then it's gon' be
white on black in the street. Then there'll be 3 million.
I tell him that.

So he writes it up, and I come off lookin' like I'm
some kinda goddamned freak, like I'm Hitler himself,
I ain't that lucky, but I got my own beauty.
It's in my steel-toed boots, in the hard corners of my shaved head.
I look in the mirror and hold up my mangled hand,
only the baby finger left. I know it's the wrong finger,
but fuck you all anyway.

I'm riding the top rung of the perfect race,
my face scraped pink and brilliant.
I'm your baby, America. Your boy.
Drunk on my own spit, I am goddamned fuckin' beautiful.
And I was born
and raised
right here.

## Morning News

Julie Chappell
Lawrence Kansas

In the blurred vision of morning
I discover that
our governor has no direction
and the 0.2 percent increase
in the Producer Price Index
has economists creaming their pants.

Hot, black coffee takes the edge off
Clinton's mental masturbation in Eastern Europe
as the first cigarette of the day
obscures the body count
in the South and East and West.
It's too bloody cold to fight in the North
unless, of course, your Celtic-Anglo
indignance gets aroused.

I light another cigarette to move on
to the Food Section where the
grimacing face of the editor panders
Midwestern Campbell's Soup béchamel
and 3-pound beef main dishes
for the Super Bowl Extravaganza

where the fans and players
cock-hard fingers stick in your face — No. 1
as they pass and fake and run
with the money from their prostitution
for that beer and truck
you can't live without.

More coffee and another cigarette
bring me news on the homefront — the humor section
where teachers are curious about
what it is they're supposed to be doing
while Romance is banned in the classroom
and Society can't decide whether the
Death Penalty is as nasty as the
Death Sentence of gray walls, plastic food,
and altered sexuality.
Or is this the Business Section?

As my coffee gets cold, and I run
out of smokes, it takes an Amazonian effort
to see another 5-Star day filled
with creativity for me
when my only desire is to make it
to the Far Side
where Truth abides
in the arrogance of a very singular immortality.

## Every Era Has Its Plague

Tamara Johnson
San Diego California

At first it seems impossible
linked as it is to risk
to being raped by a pathetic
small-time hustler
who did drugs with friends of mine
in San Francisco.

I was negative
in that window period
two weeks waiting for results
and crazy the whole time
thinking of ways to kill myself
so that no one would have to touch blood.

I feel healthy
but you don't know, do you, man
who did me like a trussed-up bird
and cancer, twice at twenty-nine,
the way to live between the space
of *no* and *yes*.

There's nothing safe about an opening.
Something in us wants to shield itself,
turn talk into a shell game,
let the blame rise fast
as *fine* can answer to
*How are you?*

Weird, and yet I think I understand
the way we act on our obsessions—
like a man I knew
past looking like a man
his hands were bandaged.
He could not stop scratching purple lesions.

I was a witness
and I stood dumb to what I saw:
only a sickbed
someone in it
waiting and fighting.
Fighting and waiting.

## Sick

Tammy Peplinski
Phoenix Arizona

I run screaming fire
in my nakedness
my white butt opening your eyes wide
afraid your precious ass might get fried?
Still I run sick inside
The cops come
tell me I'm lucky to be alive.

I wake to a man crouching at my bed
I can't see your face in the dark
(how can anyone see in the dark)
I sit up gathering blue sheets around bare legs
I ask you
how'd you get in?
(did we let you in)

You turn toward the cracked door
yellow porch light takes the shadows away
long enough to see your face
a face of indifference, of hunger, of loneliness
a face diseased, unwanted
an ugly glutinous yet impoverished face.

I ask you to go
in the silence you strike a deal
(we know there are no agreeable terms)
If I let you see my tits
you'll go your way
It's not that simple
(did we let you in)
Are you here to stay?

I picture me, flipping up my little blue top
flashing my breasts
feel sick
I don't know you
you don't know me
(that's part of the problem)
It's all too uncomfortable
Can't anyone see?

163

I'm going to be sick
(Did we let you in)
I scramble off the edge
I know if I can make it to the light I'll be all right
crossing the room feel my panties tear
stripping me,
(like apathetic voyeurs, they fall and stare)

I run screaming Fire
in my nakedness
my white butt opening your eyes wide
afraid your precious ass might get fried
Still I run sick inside
The cops come
tell me I'm lucky to be alive

America is crouching by your bed
Don't you feel lucky to be alive?

After all,
We let him inside

## Information

Tricia Warden
Jersey City New Jersey

when i hear people say

"you can't get anything for a penny."
i say a bullet,
you can get a hundred for
ninety-nine cents
they always reply
"what kind?"
i say
does it matter?
you need to shoot someone?

# Where We Live

## The Wednesday Walk

Silvana Straw
Washington DC

three madwomen live in the house
at the top of my street,
I have seen only one
and from what I can tell
she isn't mad, just scared,
and a little enthusiastic.

each morning she passes me
on her way home from buying eggs.
one morning she doesn't pass,
from her window I hear her sex
like a donkey pulling something
heavy is the sound,
scared and a little enthusiastic.

a middle-eastern girl passes
staring with her mother,
they carry canvasses and black bags,
artist stuff—the girl stares,
hoping I will notice the artists' stuff—
I imagine the canvas she carries a veil,
see the two of them before me, the air stir,
like the air around the heat of a grill,
the sootiness of skin beneath eyes,
mother looking down unaware
of what her daughter desires—
seductress, I think
she thinks of cooking me.

# Crazy

Maxwell C. Woodford
San Diego California

How many of you have a crazy next door neighbor? Well, mine is named Darren. I once had a friend named Darren, who went to Horace Mann, way back when it was still a junior high school. Every day he carried an empty cereal box to school, he would watch the movie *National Lampoon's Vacation* three or four times. His favorite part of the movie is the part where Chevy Chase wears underwear on his head. Then Darren would go get a pair of underwear to put on his head, and then he would go outside with a newspaper and a magnifying glass and his very faithful Tale-Spin cereal box and try and set the grass on fire. Once when I was in the hospital to get my appendix removed, Darren came to visit me and brought his time machine that he made out of a paper plate, and of course he took it everywhere. Darren would never wear shorts, or t-shirts. He would only wear striped shirts with long sleeves. Darren gave up his time machine for a new cereal box, the Power Rangers. This one was the whole box, but before, the Tale Spin cereal box was just the back. Eventually, Darren and his family moved to New York, where I hear everyone is weird. They rented their house to a bunch of SDSU college students. They had some wild parties before two of them got arrested, and the others couldn't pay the rent, so they were forced to leave by the authorities. I hear Darren might move back. I wonder if he still has a cereal box. Well, we'll find out.

## Maybe Mama Lion
*for Ray Manzarek*

Michael McClure
Oakland California

OH
YEAH
!   !


No,

it's *oh yeah...oh yeah...*; the wound
papered over, making paper tygers
—WITH A BANDAID . . .
BANDAIDS . . . BANDAIDS . . .

—F
E
E
L
I
N
G
*SO*
BAD!

Out of body in the blackness.
Solid silver blackness of forty billion years
—in an agony of Crazy, knowing nothing
—looking for a self to hold the mind.
BEEN THERE MANY TIMES. BEEN THERE MANY TIMES.
The sand underfoot is just a blackness
to hold the blind. Coming back to voices:
CALI, GOING BACK TO CALI, BACK TO CALI

*FORNIA*
*FORNIA,*


NOT TO THE FUR
N
A
C
E

—but to the wound!

172

Many years covered over, still deep
S
T
I
L
L
there; TRIED TO BANDAGE IT
with long stem roses and with ferns.

( (lying on the beach watching chipmunks,
watching chipmunks and BUGS
and
ODD
patterns
ON
the leaves.
HURT IN
MY SELF ES
T
E
E
M
!

( (There's a bloody war outside that's whistling
through the wound!) )

stretching
out to Someone
in
a
DREAM;
IT'S NO DREAM, STRETCHING OUT TO MAMA LION
IN A DREAM.
SO BAD! FEELING SO BAD! ALL MY FRIENDS
HAVE LEFT ME
and we're eating rich food, rich food,
with the sound of silver clinking
on the finest plates
—IN CALI, GOING BACK TO CALI—
KALI,
we're eating you
in a dream. You're a salmon.
California salmon coming back to rivers

173

revival

flowing from a head
on a cliff where folks look down on
the top of eagle's wings.

IT'S A GOOD LIFE!
IT'S A GOOD LIFE!
IT'S A GOOD LIFE!

( out of body out of mind )

—while the rain forests are coming down

IT'S A GOOD LIFE!

—while the rain forests are coming down

Hear the crashing sound

IT'S DEEP INSIDE

Your life swinging round

your body.

Does Mama Lion love you?

Does Mama Lion love you?

DOES MAMA LION LOVE YOU?

Can the salmon drown?

## Hollywoodland Part One

Danny Weizmann
Los Angeles California

These are the city lights
    shimmering like a hypnotist's pocketwatch
    in the dream dusk
These are the palm tree swinging in a swinger's paradise
This is the abandoned shopping cart
    with all of someone's worldly possessions
    rolling into the intersection
    at Beverly and La Cienega
This is the car crash
    at La Cienega and Beverly
the girl flew out the window and hit the pavement
a crowd gathered
she screamed
"Where am I?"
These are the sounds of sirens down Sunset
    chasing nightdreams and daymares
This is the afternoon hummingbird hovering gently over a
       cool
       still
       birdbath
This is the street where I walked alone
    looking for the sound and the fury
    and I got some
This is where the beheaded chicken runs its final silent yard
The neon rubber godzilla glaring mad on Hollywood Boulevard
This is fool's gold but it's real fool's gold
This is the abandoned fotomat hut
This used to be a poster store
    then it was a sushi store
    then it was a 99 cent store
    now it's another poster store
    but it's not the same posters anymore
This is planet earth
    a castaway balloon
       floating gently towards the sun
There goes the jet plane
    up in the sky
    racing like a maniac firefly
       into the web of dreams
Goodbye Hello Kitty
This is Hollywoodland

175

## Mission District Late Night

George Tirado
San Francisco California

I believe poets must really like pain.
Pain which clings to their beings like a cheap silk shirt in the rain.
Pain which drips into their souls from birth with words like
samsara karma, and quotes like
"We are born alone,"
"We live alone,"
and
"We will sure as shit die alone."
I live alone in a cheap residential hotel:
one bed,
one desk,
one sink,
the stained green carpet is covered in thoughts, words, anger,
hatred, and death.
One wall is covered in art,
the pieta holds dead son.
Sometimes I hear her cry.
But that's been played out on the blood soaked sidewalks.
Mother holds dead soldier son after gang-war claims another,
rest in peace *esay.*
It ain't enough to hide the ugliness that I call home.
I'm a Mission District poet with a cause.
Outside of my door X-covered dope dealers walk tall with
pockets filled with rock, like so much spare change and sweaty
twenty dollar bills in the other.
Packing death in his oversize low hanging Dickies he sits
crouched down drinking a forty-ounce, smoking a blunt, and
he blames everything on the white man.
Crackheads scurry from shadow to shadow to hit that pipe and
hear it sing her sweet song. And yeah, through this pain I find inspiration,
hiding, running through broken bottles, and telephone poles.
Past hookers with vacant eyes, and *Vato Locos* holding their dicks
like it's the only thing they truly own, screaming to the *cholitas,*
"Hey, mamacita."
And their homies hanging out on Mission and 24th
with their low-riding pants and spraypaint
mustaches and low, low pulled down bandanas.
They pass between themselves a bottle of Bull, a joint,
they tell stories of heroic deeds and death.

They hum and sing songs from Kid Frost, Santana, Los Lobos,
and show the day's new tattoos like an initiation into manhood.
You know Jesus, Mary, a rose, or a simple Pachuco cross
between the first finger and the thumb.
"*Carnal*, it's me, barrio homies, *por la vida*," one warrior whispers.
"*Simo'n*"
Another sign is flashed, another beer is opened.
And as I move down past all these used rigs I wish I could line them up.
They would spell out Heroin tells no fucking lies
and if you don't believe me all you have to do is ask John Belushi, Lenny Bruce,
they did it their way.
Better yet ask the woman next door, whose child was just wheeled out yesterday,
she had on fresh make-up and they did not take the blood-clotted rig out of her
cold dead blue arm.
You see, for me poetry hides everywhere.
Past smashed-out bus stop glass windows
which litter the sidewalks like unwanted glass diamond tears I saw you cry
the day you left me at some out of the way El Centro bus stop,
and you told me that you loved me and that's why you did it.
And, yeah, my pockets are empty, and the only green I know is that long shot
between the cue ball and the eight, and that ain't for sure, dig?
And blackness ain't darkness like the darkest hour before the dawn,
When night closes in and there ain't no smokes,
and one drink would be great, but a hundred might put me to sleep.
Even in the early morning dew down Mission,
and yeah George does have goosebumps
digging the quiet which is soon broken with a scream.
And I'm alone thinking of you,
memories etched deep into my mind like your crying habits
with red wine and flamenco guitars, and your pain.
And now I'm alone, and my eyes are shut
and I'm dreaming about you, but you see
dreams here in the Mission tonight
are just too damn short.

## Lousy Neighbors

Jon Longhi
San Francisco California

When we lived in the Haight there were these guys in the apartment above us who dove headfirst into the whole modern primitives thing. They had multiple body piercings, who knows what was under their clothes, and their faces alone had dozens of orifices where none should have been. When you talked to them it was really hard to keep eye contact because you'd always keep focusing in on that big dangly piece of jewelry hanging from their eyebrows or nose.

After awhile we began referring to our neighbors as the Tackle Box Faces. We made jokes about how it would take them forever to get through airport security. Even after they had filled up a bowl with earrings the little metal detector wand would keep going crazy squealing as the security guard passed it over their crotches.

The Tackle Box Faces were loud motherfuckers who played out of tune punk rock versions of the Spiderman theme song on stereos where the volume knob fell off when it was all the way up. They partied till dawn on cheap speed. I lost count of the times I woke up at three-thirty a.m. with them slam dancing on the floor over my head. If you rang their doorbell and asked them to stop they'd turn off the stereo for at least five minutes before you'd hear, *Spiderman, spiderman, does whatever a spider can...* and the jackboots would start pounding the ceiling again. When you called the cops, they never came.

I was lucky if I got three hours of sleep a night. Got where I was so exhausted all the time I almost lost my job. Couldn't focus or concentrate on anything, was always nervous and stressed out. After awhile I couldn't stand it anymore and I just snapped. I stole a piece of heavy equipment from a nearby construction site and drove it towards our building. After parking in front I maneuvered the crane so that the huge electromagnet was hanging just outside the Tackle Box Faces' livingroom window. As I hit the juice, the window erupted outwards as the TBFs flew through the air, yanked by their metal body jewelry which pulled their flesh out to thin cones. Once I had them all stuck wiggling on the electromagnet like roaches on a gluestick, I put the crane into drive and started heading towards the beach. We'd see if those jangling tallywackers could float.

# Who We Are

## Indictment

Nicole Blackman
New York New York

All I want to know is whatever happened to experimenting with drugs sex religion food cars words school alcohol America whatever happened to saying the very thing you thought you could not say whatever happened to writing a letter you knew you should not send and sending it anyway it doesn't matter whether or not you sign your name everyone knows who you are you can't even make crank calls anymore now that they have caller ID and no one buys candles anymore except Satanists and college girls trying to set the stage for romantic encounters and now they really can't talk to their mothers about sex because Mom doesn't know what a Reality condom is and she's kind of glad her daughter can't sleep around these days even though in the back of her mind she knows her baby girl might die every time she takes her clothes off but we don't have sex lives we have fax lives but we're too busy drinking coffee to think about that hell we're not even coffee achievers we're cappuccino achievers and those who yell loudest seldom vote and hepatitis is not cool heroin is not cool cancer is not cool it never was but thank god there is something that deadens our hunger keeps us skinny and makes our faces so gaunt that our eyes howl out to people on the street as if to say is it safe to go home now and where would we go half of us are living with our parents and the other half are trying to move back while saying how we're gonna drive cross country some day we don't live we just scratch on day to day with nothing but matchbooks and sarcasm in our pockets we build shrines to Lorena Bobbitt Maya Angelou and Anita Hill and all we're waiting for is something somewhere worth waiting for we shrug off labels and dismiss all of those consultants who sell our rap sheets and buying patterns to Madison Avenue all the better to sell us another chair at Ikea and we need something to kill the pain of all that nothing inside so we take Advil because it goes down like an M&M and we understand that we asked for a real future and what did we get clear beer but we fear that no one will ever understand us we fear that all we are right now is all we will ever be we fear that we don't know who the middle class is anymore we fear that pop culture is the only culture we're gonna have we open a Victoria's Secret catalog and think Oh yeah I always lounge around on the porch wearing a garter belt we fear hope because hope means doing something new our lifestyles have no life and no style we want to stop reading magazines stop watching TV stop caring about Winona Ryder movies but we are addicted to the things we hate and we can't stop going to brunch trying to start a band defending Hillary we never finish reading books we wonder why the girls behind the counter at MAC always look so mean we're making lists of new ways to say cool we never listen to the radio we never admit that America's best poem was written 40 years ago we wonder why a woman still can't get into the Citadel we never go to church but we want to be married in one someday if there is anyone left to marry then and we owe so much money to Amex we're not broke we're broken we're so poor we can't even pay attention we know that if we were born to famous parents our lives would be different we would have a show on MTV we'd be on tour we'd have licensing deals we'd be a consulting editor at Details Steven Meisel would take our portrait but it's too hard to work hard and since we weren't born into a famous family we'll just look at the fishbowls and criticize it's something to do it's quite serious it's not funny it's your life this is your fucking life we're out to lunch and we're gonna stay there our favorite childhood TV shows were made into board games and we bought them for $7 at age nine sold them for $2 at yard sales at 17 and now we're buying them all back in chic downtown stores for $20 at 25 c'mon let's get stoned and play Scooby Doo and you won't date anyone below your tax bracket you won't date anyone who lives outside your borough you won't date anyone without a job so you don't date anymore you hang out with guys girls gay straight friends sometimes sexpals and you wish they were more flamboyant so you could make allusions to Fellini or the Algonquin Round Table so you could write about them so you could finally say you wrote a goddamned screenplay so you could finally say you know what you want what do you want you want to be famous and loved and happy you want to be in Vanity Fair but you're terrified that you have nothing to offer this world nothing to say and no way to say it nothing to say but you can say it in three languages so you sell your lives over the phone to exhausted telemarketers and you wear expensive underwear under cheap clothes and the chocolate in your cup is not enough the Camel Lights in your pocket are not enough the keys on your necklace are not enough and posting messages on America Online is just the modern version of passing notes in class and you are more than the sum of the Gap Beastie Boys Spin and Kurt Cobain we loved him to death Slacker was not a major motion picture classic inertia is not an occupation and Virgin Megastore ripped off a dead rock star and is running ads that say I hate myself and I want to buy our only participation in running Washington is Rock The Vote ask not what you can do for your country ask what your country did to you and you are alternately thrilled and desperate, sky high and tucked Generation X isn't our name it wasn't even a very good book and Christian Slater isn't a spokesperson for anything he's just a bad actor with bad skin it is way past your dead time cigarettes make it easy to talk so let me make it easy for you these are the bad old days don't shit where you sleep don't fuck where you don't stay you keep playing you're played out so let's quit walking through Lollapalooza looking for fun a soulmate a reason to live a new $20 t-shirt let's pretend that a haircut will save us so let's pretend that compassion is cool let's get rid of the X-girl t-shirts tattoos chain wallets rollerblades baby barrettes and backpacks let's pretend that we actually know how much money we made last year let's stop listening to white boys talk about all the crack babies they never saw the black girls they never met the drugs they never did what are you gonna write on your tax return under occupation cynical fucker quit whining that you haven't done anything wrong cause you haven't done much of anything so let's talk about how we don't listen to Madonna's records but we really admire her gift for self-promotion let's complain about our butts let's get a membership at the gym let's never go to the gym let's talk about how we never go to the gym let's make dysfunctional families sound neat let's have another Rolling Rock let's get drunk let's stay drunk let's do drugs let's go into recovery let's talk about recovery let's recover from recovery Yoko Ono is so out she's in so Fluxus this motherfuckers all we want is a head rush all we want is to get out of our skin for a while we have nothing to lose because we don't have anything anything we want anyway we used to hate people now we just make fun of them it's more effective so let's stop arguing and start the car let's quit writing suicide notes on deposit slips let's stop procrastinating and write that book we've been carrying inside for 25 years let's admit that America gets the celebrities she deserves let's stop pretending that we understand jazz let's look at two beautiful people kissing and pretend that one of them is us let's stop saying don't quote me because if no one quotes you then you probably haven't said anything worth saying let's stop pretending that there isn't a difference between being alone and lonely let's stop pretending that this doesn't hurt let's stop praying for someone to save us and start saving ourselves let's stop this and start over let's go out let's keep going.......

## Avocado Toilets

Matt Cook
Shorewood Wisconsin

We saw this avocado colored toilet in the street one day
It was one of those days
   when people were putting things in the street
We came up with this idea to put this avocado colored toilet
In the back of this guy we didn't like's truck
So we went and we found this guy's truck
And we put this avocado colored toilet
Right in the back of this guy's truck
Had a good laugh about it
Forgot about it
A year goes by    we're driving around again
We see another avocado colored toilet
Just like before    virtually identical
So we go and we find that guy's truck again
And we put this avocado colored toilet
Right in the back of his truck again
We just kept putting things in his truck
We thought it would send him on an emotional rollercoaster
But it didn't work
He was too well-adjusted
It didn't phase him
He thought they were just green toilets
That's why he was a guy we didn't like

## Celluloid, Food and Drugs

Clebo Rainey
Dallas Texas

Celluloid, food and drugs.
America runs on these three items.
They attach themselves to our wheels
    as we rush into our toxic future.
The Indians that have always been here to begin with
    come out of the woodwork
    as darkness sweeps the city.
And the chase begins.
It spins us into spiral landings
    on uncharted territories
    of our own shared subconscious.
We all learn to never say never
    and keep on searching the video racks
    and the food shelves
    and the drug dealing alleys
    for what we all seek
    like some kind of primitive insects.
There are mirrors everywhere for our society it seems
    but nothing beams us in on the truth
    like our stomachs
    our imaginations
    or our sensual selves.
My lover sits in front of the TV
    searching for a news show
    about the effects of radiation fallout
    in the Soviet Union
    for a quiet evening of viewing entertainment.
The babies' brains born there are glowing green
    like the dollars' nuclear energy saves them.
They will grow up to be luminescent glowing consumers
    of industrial waste.
The drug dealer's new car screeches down the street
    and my stomach starts to growl.
A howl goes off somewhere in the distance
    as another junkie ODs from fat
    or greed
    or too much video consumption.
The multicolored colors of Noemi's crayons
    begin to draw pictures in the sand

of my own devilish hands
wrecked hard by the gunboats of past lovers
and drug deals gone weird.
She only stops to eat some angel food cake
and sugar coated strawberries
she pours over our copy of Videodrome
and lights some incense
to cover the smell of drugs.
We slip into the slipstream of our own shock waves
and blast forward to our own death
in a fast car
full of celluloid... food... and drugs.
Suddenly it starts to rain
a black smelly gooey rain outside
that eats into the car like acid.
We grab each other for one last kiss
spinning out of control
as our car tumbles end over end
and out comes the celluloid, food and drugs
all holding our souls down to the earth
where we are all doomed to life
here in the poison prisons
where we are all the jailers
the jailed
and even the builders of the jail
where the smell has grown foul
and somewhere in the distance
another ambulance howls
like death...
or passion...
or both.

## Slack Angst 1 & 2

Randy Blazak
Atlanta Georgia

i'm bug-eyed on the mac
gen spin docs say i'm slack
cornelius wasn't a monkey
reagan was a high dollar flunkie
had a lunch box made out of metal
adam 12 stars, space sticks and a glass bottle
g.i. joe used to be big
charlotte was the spider not the pig
saw hank aaron hit a homer
price is right girls gave me a boner
heard crazy tales about alice cooper
bought a now & later from mr. hooper
73 gran torino like starsky & hutch
it didn't have the stripe or the clutch
waiting tables with a master's degree
rocket in my pocket's gotta be p.c.
tattoo love chicks with pierced tongues
joey ramone ministry for the young
new-rock nostalgia too soon
52 girls and 99 luftbaloons
still want to kill mark david chapman
forgot 1986, just what happened
saw my life sold as a trend in details
rolfed a tuna for the gay baby whales
eurailed through southern france
got the wrong garanimal on my pants
watergate meant grown-ups were liars
jumped the snake river canyon on my huffy wildfire
had two dates like peter brady
slow dance make-out to "who's that lady"
got a low impact job
all praise to bob
dorm room trip to the paisley underground
3:00 bangle sent me california bound
rent checks underwritten by kroger shoplifting
firehose t-shirts that are loose fitting
glad i don't need religion
glad i don't eat pigeons
survived the unforgettable fire

don't know where to recycle my tire
don't fear a black planet
fear the family of janet
grabbed my crotch
lost my swatch
fed the world with a song
discovered the goddess in a thong
pretend the cable is free
i need clues on which life to lead
go ballistic moshin'
actin' like i'm still steve austin
if i had a kid
i'd name him sid
always hated that hacky-sack
got beat up playing billy jack
got a slurpee kiss cup and a wacky pack
got a hundred miles of hot wheel track
got a skinny tie when i got the knack
scratched my dad's 45 of "sugar shack"
wonder who is the mack
shoot hoops like john concack
my neighbor's smokin' crack
boss with a cross full of gack
dr. spock was a quack
chicks give me flack
want my hippity-hop back
wanna snap back like stanbac
keep my LPs in a stack
buy my suits of the thrift store rack
drink coffee for the speed i lack
got me hummin' like a rayovac
in my mind there is no slack

# X

Stephen Spyrit
Portland Oregon

generation at the completion of the alphabet
listening to the christening of the label
crystalize on you now you're through.
Connie and Dan have
explained a generation away in the shotgun
blast motif. is that x as in used to be guys?
Generation xtinct as in the lie that doesn't fit
anymore. not that it's replaced by a new truth it's
kinda like amputation x marks the spot.
the spot that is a hole that generation W fell into
chasm where ideals let loose their grip
they fell into the pit of credit.
X-ray the xuberant xploiters of the letter generation
generation V the purveyors of plutonium WW2
crying at generation W about 'their' children.
Passage of the xplorers of apathy
anarchy alchemically fused in lives.
Chaos' children are the last to listen
elders remembering pre-electricity,
sight by flame.
Xpensive discovering that cash, material gain
cannot xplain xcuse or xorcise the demon truths in the
lie.
Gen W tried to balance use moderation on the xtreme
actions
xciting them. the Y children now hitting the planet
petrify
V and W. they make X look silly. They are well armed
ascended
and taking no generational backwash
Xpect from X no xclusions it's not a thing of
generations anymore.

## Guilty, with Explanation

Paul D. Dickinson
St. Paul Minnesota

Suddenly, there has been a change of plans. I'm in Chicago with a knife at my throat. Unstabbed, I stumble away and find my discarded license a few blocks down – I'm smiling at the camera. When I got back into town, my going-away party had already started. I went down to the tracks. I knelt down and put my ear to the cold rail. I heard it and then I saw it, crossing the Mississippi, coming toward me. At the last minute, I jumped out of the way. It thundered past me, loud, strong, without apology. Outside the convenience store, an old man stares at me. I chew my gum and carefully stare back. He finally speaks: "When I was your age, I didn't do shit." Nothing, I think, can kill me now.

## We Are The Dinosaur

Bob Holman
New York New York

Blast open the gates to kingdom come
Whoops what happened to everyone
Planted a seed_Grew into a gun
Dum de dum dum dum dum dum dumb

Life is a riot livin in a cartoon
Ice-age in a dumpster—that's our living room
Set fire to your roof—get a better view
Global warming is a warning—toodle-oo

We are the dinosaur
We don't live here anymore
We got what we were askin for
Follow the dinosaur

Ho ho homo sapiens
Ain't so smart
Ka ka kamikaze, Friend
Which way is the ark?

The world is dialin 911
The don't walk sign just changed to you better run
What we are waiting for has long since come
Dum-de-dum dum dumm dum dum

Cross the scorchin sands with my big fat feet
It's hard becoming diesel fuel with nothin to eat
Better catch us quick—we're outta here
We're pre-winged birds & tend to disappear

We are the dinosaur
We don't live here anymore
We got what we were asking for
Follow the dinosaur

Hurry, disappear! Back to the Past!
Did you really think the Future was gonna last?
It's endin with a bang so let's have a blast
Let's dine cannibal—it makes a nice contrast

Chauffeured ambulances race to the prom
Santa, please bring me a neutron bomb
Recycle the planet before the earth is a grave
But please excuse me—I gotta get back to my cave

We are the dinosaur
We don't live here anymore
We got what we were askin for
Follow the dinosaur

T-t-take a chance
It's all a joke
M-m-m-may I have this dance
Th-that's all folks

## Bull By The Horns

Todd Colby
Brooklyn New York

Taking the bull by the horns
And lifting the bull up by the horns
And taking the bull by the horns
And taking the bull up by the horns
And lifting the bull by the horns up into the air
Taking the bull up by the horns and lifting it into the air
The bull is hoisted into the air by the horns
The bull is caught by the horns
The bull is taken by the horns and tossed into the air
The bull is caught
The bull is caught by the horns and tossed kicking into the air
Just lifting the bull up by the horns and tossing it into the river
To just throw the bull into the river by the horns
To just throw the bull a long way
To just toss the bull away
To take the bull by the horns and throw it kicking into the river
Kicking and screaming and snorting
And not being upset that the bull is upset that it is being
Taken by the horns and is dripping goo from the ring in its nose
And the bull is snorting and making wild sounds and taking the bull
By the horns anyway and tossing it into the river
To just throw the bull into the river
To just throw the bull a very long way
Because you want the bull out of your life
The kicking and screaming and snorting bull is in the river
You wanted the bull the fuck out of your life so you took it
By the horns and tossed it into the river
You took the bull by the horns
You caught the bull by the horns
You stood next to the river
You lifted the bull by the horns over the fence next to the river
You tossed the bull in the water by the horns
You wanted the bull the fuck out and now it's the fuck out
It's a long way to toss a bull but you did it
You took it by the horns
I hope you're happy
I hope you are very happy
I hope you're wonderfully happy and having a good time watching
The bull in the water

You tossed the bull into the water by the horns
You watched the hooves thrashing in the air and the water and its
Horns bobbing and I hope you have a very pleasant day
A wonderfully pleasant day
And a happy and a very pleasant and a very happy day.

## I Don't Care

Henry Alarmclock
Denver Colorado

"I don't care," said Pierre, the voice of his generation.

"I don't care," stuck in midair, and folded his arms w/a sneer. I don't care I'm going downstairs where the wonderful bottles are stored—down there and get me some golden stuff, drink it w/my eyes closed. Downstairs w/my eyes closed I don't care if my guts are boiling down where Granpappy keeps the rye whiskey, and sit there, and never move, arms folded like a sullen French schoolboy, and my whole generation too.

My sadness kind of a sad unknowing—slicked-back hair I don't care. Wanting somehow to be mothered and borne up away from my lonely discomfort. Some safe harbor to launch from, and go back into at the end of each long evening's battles.

And the waitress w/black hair, she don't care. And the bums in the alley, they don't. Blunk, like a non-word made up, found, or discovered in head, which might not mean anything, actually doesn't or if so, I don't care. Spare me your golden reproach.

So what I gotta crack in my head, and not even God can tame me. Down in the basement where holy golden bottles are, and yum honey, suck, gulp—Mind already inside the hot fruit. So what I'm still young man in this life, capable and full of opening worlds—I expect you pardon me my apathy. See What Happens is all, and don't get hung up. Summer again, and comparing vaginas to flowers— oh well so what I don't care—I gulp the golden bottles.

I don't care a joyful noise before the Lord—some odd, detached assurance very centered indeed, good. Giggling tee hee haw I have a psychache. Following legs and asses down the mall in hot fry heat, in a dose, in a trance, sidewalk hot enough to fry a brain on. Street cynicism disproven I don't care.

I and the Gypsies we don't care. I and the Peaceful Dolls. The Blessed Ones are going onstage. Who will be our next victim? Who will not care next, by cause of our devious influence?

People drive themselves mad in circles

around and around forever

CARING so much about everything—red eyes, hearts and emotions flaring, everyone

CARING—what why when who next—look at em go! They remind me of the halfwit, Jimmy, maliciously cracking corn in the face of intended stillness. Fighting wars and building shopping malls everywhere and sinister, computerized "information superhighways"—armored cops and superintelligent laser-equipped flying tanks w/wings faster than the wings of angels—

I'm talking about not caring in a BEAUTIFUL way. I'm talking about the giggling buddies of agreement you'd find everywhere, in every doorway huddled together over Holy Smoke—the GOLDEN Way—if nobody cared. Means I BELIEVE in Us, and the coming inevitable Victory of the Young Light (so why wring hands and worry?)

I don't care I don't care I don't care

I have fleeced and denied them all. Aging policeman followed by female dogcatcher—spare me your golden reproach.

Arise, you rabble, I have wrested these apples from the toppermost branches of the tallest trees—and lay them before you now for all to share, a row of rosy, joyous apples—I DARE you to taste them.

## As Ye Sow, So Shall Ye Reap

Elyse
San Diego California

don't give me all of your neat and tidy
rules I am the weed I thrive
in that crack in the sidewalk
of your brain I bloom
in spite of chemical warfare against me
curl and grip
my roots 'round the hardness
of your heart choke
your landscaping sleep
in the bed you made for another
flower in the fierce hotness
of your deepest denied desires
and you curse me
douse me with gasoline I am
beautiful and you
stab at me with scissors
chop me with your axe you cannot
see my beauty with your dagger eyes
nor revel in my scent
with turned up nose I'd rather
keep company with a parking meter
more ready and willing to make change
than you insisting
on your way with Mother
Earth I've known her longer
than you children
call me Dandelion.

## How I Am Defined By American Heritage
(Emphasis Mine)

Lauri Conner
Seattle Washington

*I am*
    of the color Black
    producing
reflecting comparatively
    little light
dark
    in color
solid
  as from soot
dirty extreme
    of the neutral gray
  having no predominant hue
    *I am*
    marked
by anger and
incurring censure
  *while*
appearing to emanate from a source
  other
that the actual point
    of origin
for reasons of security
*I* respond to
zero stimulation not
  to be suppressed
*from your*
conscious recognition
that plays games
with
  colored pieces
like chess or
  checkers
*I am*
    evil
    wicked
prohibiting dissemination of
    *something*

attended with disaster
   that is not served
with milk
   or cream

*I am*
   an adult
   female
   human being
   someone
   colored
   black

## Rasta Not

Tracie Morris
New York New York

I wear these dreads
Repped crown of thorns
Upon my head
but do not mourn
the lion's tread.
I'd rather scorn
the lie that lead
my others born
to fancy. Fled
pressed kinks forlorn
napping not dead
tied — roots untorn.

## Drunk Like a Frog

Allan Wolf
Asheville North Carolina

It's when your life falls to sleep and you are brain-dead and all that's left is your heart like a Bull Frog alone on a pond and every possibility eases past on the water and there you are on your lily pad in the dark, croaking.

Inside, you ask: "Is this the way I'm meant to be? Is this still pond my Paradise? Am as apathetic as I seem?" Outside yourself you manage only low and plunky moans, floating on the surface in a slow-going circle.

Apply your bulgy eyes to the sight of striders gliding graceful all around and (as they do their delicate dance to taunt your thick and graceless mass) it hits you how easy those of no substance can walk upon water which

makes you jealously seek solace in the fact that you can eat them and you do so, one by one, with your undeniable tongue, then you plunge in search of nourishment beneath the bumbling awkward surface

and there take part in graceful frog ballets, amphibious tangos, web-footed contra dances, "into the center with a whoop an' a holler" you glow and twirl like Esther Williams and, my God, you are so beautiful.

## Death of the ...

Wammo
Austin Texas

It was easy. Easy to hit my thumb with a hammer and calendar the great black spot caterpillaring across my nail until the whole sucker just fell right off. It was easy to take the blows and hold back the tears, pummeled by bullies for being the new kid in a small Texas town. It was easy to chomp at the bit, feel the sting of the lash and take you warm and dark into my mouth. But this? This social function, where the spiders crawl in designer clothes. All strangers except your lover, who knows everyone else. This empty pit. A seething mass of facade and pomp. Cold in soulless, claw sharpened fluff. This...

## PARTY

Oh, I guess I could play the game and I guess I'll end up doing so but for now, I'll take solace in the fact that this situation inspires me to write. I'm anywhere but here. I'm spending the entire evening in bed. Alone. Drinking wine. Jerking off. Sending out for pizza and reading until I fall asleep. I'm cruising the drag in an old beat up Fairlane convertible, cranking Scratch Acid or Jesus Lizard and watching the young, lithe, even tanned bodies of the little college boys and girls. I'm spending the entire day under water in Barton Creek. Waiting for night to kiss the world like a dark jewel and emerge from my bubble screaming, "ALRIGHT, LET'S TORCH THIS MANGY TOWN!"

That's the time for life. Born in the dark with your eyes wide like a bat or a fox. Dancing in the violet crisp evening air to your own music. Instead I'm trapped in this gayly lit smoke filled room, scowling. Wincing at the forced laughter and the catty whines. "So and so's such a bitch..." and "That director sucks..." and "This actor sucks that director." While that sterile euro disco popsicle shit on a stick mindless programmed crap shoots out of the speakers like dirty tainted jizz. JICKA JICKA KAH... JICKA JICKA KAH... MENNA MENNA MENNA MENNA MENNA MENNA... music so clean, it makes my teeth feel scraped. I want to throw up my guts and run around the room. Strangling each guest with my entrails. Drawing pictures on the walls with my own blood and shit. But no, I'll just stand here looking stupid. Drinking a Colorado fascist light beer, I found in a sparkling fridge filled with zima and pate and diet soda until...

It, the death of the party. It, the disco MTV jello mold beast. It sees me. Its hair is perfect. Its skin is perfect. Its clothes are perfect. Its brain is a turd and it's swaggering mincingly straight towards me. THIRTEEN STEPS. FLOORLESS JIG. ANYTHING BUT THAT.

## Ode to Torment

David Kunian
New Orleans Louisiana

I've seen
what I want to be
when I grow up:

She was only
the second man
I've wanted to fuck.
Torment—

The punk rock drag queen.
Jet black hair,
wooden platform clogs
with towering inferno heels
Aflame she struts
with more attitude
than every Lollapaloozer
on that side of the sound board.
The glorious trash
came out of her mouth
Masturbation, fornication
"If you could suck your own dick
would you ever leave the house?"

To the tight-sphinctered jocks
sponsored by Coors Light,
the attitude came and came
the usual fast and furious.
They dropped two G's on her
"Yeah, no shit I'm a fag."
At the end of the day,
Torment stripped
and revealed her secrets
that most clam divers can't conceive,
showing exactly what was under her hair.
Above catcalls and cheers,
He stood stark on stage,
eyes steady,
        "I could be anyone
        of you."

In this City That Forgot To Care
we constantly scale
the heights of ignorance.
We need more Torment
because TORMENT RULES!

## Twentynothing

Jeff McDaniel
Washington DC

Most kids my age slack on their ass. Not me.
I begin each day with a little project.

Today, I'm gonna give myself a black eye
in every family photograph.

My loony grandmother's coming to visit.
She's got big holes in her mind.

There I am in your backyard, Grandma, right after
you cracked me in the face with the end of a rake.

All I wanted was a Pepsi.
I can't believe you don't remember.

Here I go at my seventh birthday party, when
you knocked some sense into me with a frying pan.

You were drunk. When you sang happy birthday
you referred to me as the mistake. I'll never forget that.

Don't cry, Grandma. I forgive you. For a hundred bucks.
When my father gets home, I'll tell him: she did it.

Dad, she went through every family photo album
with a black pen and drew tiny bruises beneath my eyes.

Only your credit card can alleviate the pain.
I'll never make as much money as him. .

I'm twentynothing—the distance between a headline
and where our heroes explode,

twentynothing—the time it takes to slide a condom
over the barrel of a handgun,

twentynothing—the remainder of television
over phone sex multiplied by divorce,

twentynothing—the chances of a snowball surviving
the inevitable nuclear hell,

twentynothing—the number of syllables
in the word: disease,

twentynothing—the grimace the brain makes
when confronted with our crater in history.

I'm not lazy like most punks my age,
and I've got a diary to prove it.

Monday: scheduled root canal surgery with every dentist
in San Francisco, which isn't even my time zone.

Tuesday: mailed bomb threats to every Denny's branch
in America—switch to Dr. Pepper by sunset or else!

Wednesday: sat on my rooftop with a shotgun
and pulverized faxes zipping in from Europe.

Thursday: belched in the face of a smiling
toll booth lady for good luck.

I'm a religious guy. Like Benjamin Peret says
if I see a priest being beaten, I make a wish.

Since ejaculation is a prayer reduced to its simplest
expression I consider myself deeply spiritual.

Recently I had a transcendental experience.
It was like *uuugghh* with a British accent.

## Divine Symphony of the Damned

Bucky Sinister
San Francisco California

Hard grind for a hard time
There's so much to feel
So little time

Pain don't mean nothing anymore
A laugh don't mean nothing anymore
Bodily functions don't mean nothing anymore
No regurgitation
No defecation
No pigeons pecking at your spit on a hot day
    and you can't figure out why you feel so cold

There's no time to figure out why
You've got little time to live
You've got little reason to live
You've got less reason to die

Reason doesn't mean anything
    when a madman plucks discordant strings
    and makes the world go round
The divine symphony of the damned plays on
    and there you are in the crescendo
The music your life makes
    is just another thing you hate
    that you have no power to change

The neighbors complain that the music's too loud
    but the volume knob is nowhere to be found
    and you have no time to look for it.
    There's no time to learn the words
    no time no reason to play air guitar
    with a razor blade
Just slam down that gas pedal and drive
Suffocate that gas pedal and drive

Put on Pink Floyd
    because it's just like you
Put on the White Album
    because it's just like you

Put on Black Flag
    because it's just like you
Put on Skinny Puppy
because it's just like you
Steve Albini is your mother singing you to sleep
    when a rubber room devil is laughing in your ear.

You can scream as loud as clenched teeth will allow
    but it won't take the white from your knuckles
    or the red wildness out of your eyes
You can scream as loud as clenched teeth will allow
but it won't make your drugs work any better
    it won't make anyone love you
    it won't make your prayers reach the ears of your gods
You can scream as loud as clenched teeth will allow
and you can kick your head back
    and open your mouth as wide as you can
    let your screams explode out
    and travel to the sun to be swallowed
    and then you'll discover that
    you will need another mouth or two
    to scream as loud as you want
So what's the point?
No reason to scream,
No time to learn to scream louder.

But look for the guy by the side of the road
with no arms and no legs
hitchhiking with his tongue—
that will be me.
Stop, pick me up, give me a ride,
and together we will scream loud enough
    to make the wind stop blowing
Together we will scream
    the music we cannot get away from
Together we will scream
    the blue right out of the sky
And when the brakes go out at the top of the hill
    it will be all you can do to steer.

# Nerds

Jeff 'Shappy' Seasholtz
Chicago Illinois

HEY YOU— you well dressed corporate ASS KISSER with your CAR PHONE and your FIL-O-FUX

we're comin' for you.

AND YOU— joggin' by in those $200 running shoes and that DISC-MAN sittin' on your $40 haircut

we're comin' for you.

AND ALL YOU FUCKIN STEROID CASES— you used to snap us in the ass with your wet towels in gym class and put your smelly JOCK STRAPS on our heads for a laugh

we're comin' for you.

WE ARE THE BROTHERHOOD
AND WE ARE STRONG
WE ARE THE BROTHERHOOD
OF THOSE WHO DIDN'T BELONG
WE ARE THE BROTHERHOOD OF NERDS
AND THE TABLES HAVE BEEN TURNED
NERDS, MOTHERFUCKER!

NO LONGER SHALL WE BE SPURNED

while you were playing in your LITTLE LEAGUE
WE were playing DUNGEONS & DRAGONS

When you were at that VAN HALEN concert
WE were listening to DEVO and drawing pictures of androids
and when YOU were at your stupid HIGH SCHOOL PARTIES
drinking your dad's beer and KICKIN' EACH OTHERS ASSES
WE WERE STILL PLAYING DUNGEONS & DRAGONS

OH HOW YOU PRETTY BOYS loved to TAUNT US
HUMILIATE US for your AMUSEMENT
little did you realize HOW STRONGER WE BECAME

WE designed ALL the computer programs
you use in your CORPORATE PRISON
so COMPLICATED that by the time you
UNDERLINGS figure out our programming
WE CHANGE IT
IMPROVE IT
MAKING IT IMPOSSIBLE FOR YOU TO COMPREHEND
and when your terminal breaks down
YOU ARE AT OUR MERCY
AND THOSE "GEEKS" in the marching band
are PRODUCING and PLAYING all of your
favorite ALTERNATIVE MUSIC

AND MAKE NO MISTAKE ABOUT IT— WE HAVE YOUR WOMEN!
as you rot away in your self-induced CORPORATE COME
drink lite beer and watching MONDAY NIGHT
FUCK-BALL
WE ARE MARCHING ONWARD
your women are bored by your inability to
think about anything else
besides sport scores and
STOCK-MARKET VALUES RISING UP YOUR FAT ASS

WE can seduce your women with our intellect
with our knowledge of things YOU deemed NERDY

"HA-HA," you laugh, "WOMEN TAKE ONE LOOK AT MY MUSCLE BOUND FEATURES
AND GO FRIGGIN' NUTS!"

well, little DAVID COPPERFIELD sat in his basement practicing card tricks and
GUESS WHAT? HE'S shuffling Schiffer's deck!

PUDGY BILLY JOEL tinkled on his little toy piano and got himself a
subscription to SPORTS ILLUSTRATED that you can only DREAM ABOUT, FUCK-O!

AND AS WE MOVE INTO THE NEXT CENTURY
YOU will be trapped in your JUST DO IT
WHY ASK WHY mentality while the
BROTHERHOOD OF NERDS snaps YOU
in the ASS with the wet towel of
INNOVATION and we'll have a hearty chuckle at your expense while
PLAYING DUNGEONS & DRAGONS IN OUR VIRTUAL REALITY BASEMENTS!

NERRRDZ!

## Alternative Fashion

Jennifer Joseph
San Francisco California

"You look like you're dressed for a tea party," she said semi-snidely, insinuating that I wasn't dressed grunge enough for the occasion, which was in fact a day-long outdoor concert in the middle of summer, insinuating that somehow by wearing a dress (god forbid) I had committed some incredible faux pas, broken some unwritten law, because alternative culture isn't really that alternative when it comes to fashion. The rules are strict and if you're wearing anything but black then forget it, you're a hopeless nerd, a fashion don't, regardless of whether it's 100 degrees without a cloud in the sky and the sun is beating down relentlessly like the ozone layer never existed, and it's by far the flimsiest piece of clothing you own, and everyone who is wearing black is baking away in their own personal micro-crisp, and whatever happened to individuality anyway? It's like someone'll dye their hair purple to be different and then all their friends think it's cool so they dye their hair too and then everybody's the same; and it's true for tattoos too - they're *so* tribal - now we're all members of the same tribe. Why not just get a barcode tattooed on your forehead and forever have fun making the machine go berserk as you scan yourself at the checkout line? I mean, goddamit, if I want to wear a dress, I'm gonna go ahead and wear a dress, and frankly I don't care what my goddam hair is doing, and would someone please tell me what's so alternative about a fuckin black tee shirt with some band's name on it that costs 20 bucks?

## Skinny

Beth Lisick
San Francisco California

Here, skinny. Here, skinny, skinny, skinny. It's suppertime, skinny. Time to eat now.

Mmmm. Frosty hair-does, glossy-lipped, mini-skirted, Executanned mallbaby. With your coral polished toenails just shoved into scuffed white pumps. Size number six. Have you got a tattoo of a rose on your skinny little peach bottom? Or maybe just a gold ankle bracelet?

Here, skinny. Come on now, little skinnyskinnyskinny.

New wave skinny with your sassy jet black bob, kohl-lined eyes, push-up bra, velvet flares, platforms on sale from NaNa, and a chunky, junky ring on your index finger. Now some days you feel like wearing that mole, and some days you don't. I mean, whatsername does it. And that's okay! You, too, can reinvent your image seasonally, skinny.

George Carlin did some concert for HBO about the same time the sensitive afterschool specials and People magazine covers were tackling the American girl's favorite new disease. But he said, rich cunt, won't eat, fuck her.

Oh, skinny. Listen to me now, skinny. Over here, skinnyskinnyskinny.

Vegan granola girl won't eat my whole wheat Fig Newtons cause they got too many ingredients in them. She's pushing the seat on her Volkswagen bug way back so she's got father to hit the clutch.
"You burn more calories that way."

"I don't know why I'm puking," she says. "It must be something I ate."

Gosh, it must be. Ben and Jerry's, Oreo, ranch-style, sour cream & onion, fruit pie, feel like chicken tonight! It must be something you ate.

Oh, pretty girl, soft girl, sweet girl, smart girl, sophisticated girl.

You big-ass lying tramp, tacky gold digging nymphomaniac, menstruating manhating dictator, insecure anorexic manipulator. Come here, now.

Come on, skinny. On, please, skinnyskinnyskinnyskinny.
That's a good girl! Heel! Sit! Roll over! Now play dead.

Rich cunt. Won't eat. Fuck her.

## She Was So Bad

Pleasant Gehman
Los Angeles California

She was so bad
that when she walked down the hallways at school
the whispers and stifled giggles preceded her like a hurricane
she wore black leatherette hotpants
and black vinyl lace-up boots, her hair was dyed black
she wore her boyfriend's faded denim jacket
because it matched her eyes and the shadow she wore in wings
that nearly reached her ears
She was so bad
she cracked her gum
talked back to everyone
teachers and policemen alike
smoked in front of her mother, swore at her father
and carried a condom foil-wrapped in her wallet
before it was acceptable for girls to do so
She was so bad
as bad as her marks, as bad as her complexion
worse than they all thought
but she didn't care what they thought
she didn't care when she got caught shoplifting
earrings and nail polish from Woolworth's
she cared about her appearance though
in the same way pimps and gangsters do
the day she became my idol
she dragged a turquoise chair all the way across the cafeteria
because the orange one she'd been sitting in
clashed with her outfit
She was so bad

## Circus Train Wreck

Melody Jordan
Portland Oregon

Once there was a girl who thought that she was baby-sitting
but she wasn't she was making a turkey
Once there was a man who stood in the doorway
of the girl who slept facing the wall
she turned around he was gone she chased him down the hall
yelling, "If a boy was molested by clowns was he ever really there at all"
and they found giraffes in Oklahoma
some sort of circus train wreck you know
Once there was this girl who thought that if
she could just say it loud enough
if she could just say it fast enough
if she could just get it out somehow
once there was doctors who said that someone was lying
that someone could not play piano
Lock me outside naked make me take showers with my clothes on
LIESLIESLIAR
that's not you you're the cover up

# On The Road (Again)

## Motorists, Do Not Be Fooled

Jim Stewart
Albuquerque New Mexico

do not be fooled, you are not down yet
though it seemed utah would never end, and it's hard to believe
     it's on the same planet
floating over pink oceans of sandstone
under cheap neon whites and purples of river-flood carved mesas
climbing the Virgin Mountains
around rollercoaster hills over the rise and into the set of a
     Roadrunner cartoon dawn exploding out from between concealing
     rough blasted-rock walls

do not be fooled though it all turned green in Colorado, & trailer
     parks and exits when after Selina it was 150 miles of desert
     and you
with cornnuts and Texaco coffee for breakfast and billboard ads for
     dinner
and you made it to a gas station with a gallon left in the tank
and it's all getting easier, pulled down like with a magnet to
     Denver, you are not down yet

because the caffeine is letting you close your eyes against the
     acid pools in your gut and leg cramps and spazzing lower back
     around the kidney
you've done the nod-and-wink three times and anyone who could take
     the wheel is just as tired too
and the crackheads on the Denver streets want to talk to you
offer you drugs, slit your throat
do not be fooled

because it's a 6-percent grade twister of a ride from here on in
     with hot brakes and diarrhea and the semis slam you with walls
     of air and the earth rolls you out from under the bleary sun
     and you are not down yet

## Mental Traffic

Julia Delbridge
Radford Virginia

The wind from
Eighteen wheels of existential,
metaphysical, transcendental questions
Thundering by at 80 miles per hour
Blows me over, out of my lane

Grandma's algebraic Impala
Blocks both lanes and makes me late
Should have risen earlier

A poetic school bus
Smiles and waves in passing
Laughing

Weekend off ramp
Winds around and back again
Pistons ping
Monday morning cold start
Add a quart of midnight oil
Adjust the timing
Of this rusty
Sixty-three

Wishing it could be a supercharged
Turbo-injected space mobile
Like the one that just flew by

Or a motorcycle, spirit-free
Of this rusted, dented body
But it runs
And only occasionally breaks down
Then junkyard parts add character
And it's paid for

## Runaway Van

Michael Salinger
Cleveland Ohio

Apparently this vehicle never had rear brakes
A fact
Denied
Masked
An autocidal tendency repressed
By two discs and four opposed shoes
Up front
Working overtime
A little pressure maybe some pumping and we
would glide
To a controlled stop
Safely
Nothing risked
Dependable transportation
On the surface she seemed a safe ride
And I was comfortable with this arrangement
Four thousand pounds of glass and steel reinforced
Complacency
I trusted her with my life
A little extra pressure rhumba seat goosing fluid
From the master cylinder
Shaking through copper tubes
Spider twisted beneath the undercarriage
And with every thrust a bit of juice slips through
A crack in the brake line
A little bit of pressure and the gap grows
unperceived
Every time
15 degree grade
A gentle depression receives no response
Multiple foot stomps receive no response
A desperate grab for the emergency brain receives
no response
Three foot ditch leap
Bi tired Spanky Spangler Evel Kneivel and Super
Dave Osbourne
Roll caged into one maneuver
AIR BORN
AIR BORN

Look Ma I'm flying
I'm flying
Ultra Brite Close Up Colgate knuckles
Road map veins bursting up overinflated fore
arms
In a steering wheel do or die
Death grip
LOOK MA I'M FLYING
Three or four pointless landings
Wheatfield racing through maple saplings
Through points of strobe light
Flashes
A thousand points of reference
But still
I find time to count the leaves on the trees
Ten thousand thoughts ricochet off the guardrails
of my skull
Til finally we stop
Resting in a nest of branches and briars
My heart moth yellow light bulb bouncing
Inside my chest
And I can't decide
Whether this ride
Was worth the mess

## How It Cost Me 10 Times As Much As Anyone Else to Get Into Lollapalooza For Free

Jennifer Gleach
Portland Oregon

I fell in love and flipped my car in the same week. The car, she's totaled — the boy, we'll see. I'm just glad he didn't want anything to do with Lollapalooza—so I was by myself when I hit the gravel at 50 m.p.h. That's the state trooper's guess. My old crush, he didn't want to go either and I knew better than to ask Adam. Some other writer guy found out at the last minute that he, too, could be a stadium poet—but by then I just wanted to go solo, think about love and memorize my new words, and be nervous in peace and quiet.

So, I'm driving alone and talking out loud, middle of nowhere, middle of the night—mile marker 45, Rt. 97 north. There's orange sign after orange sign, but no sign of construction so the warnings didn't register. I missed the one that said loose gravel ahead and missed the 15 M.P.H. — CAUTION — almost missed PAVEMENT ENDS — but it caught my eye just as I saw the ledge itself and skipped like a jumpy needle on that Trigger cut single over the solid edge. It felt like a cliff for a second, then the fishtailing (an action which is exactly what the word portrays) and down in a ditch up a slight rise. We went over on the driver's side and landed on the roof in the soft desert ground anchored with fierce sharp dry brush. The roof on the ground and my feet pointed at the roof.

Go figure. My life didn't pass before my eyes, it wasn't slow motion and I did not have any big "I WANNA LIVE!!!" urges nor did I say my prayers assuming my number was up. No, just like the car didn't catch on fire, my feelings weren't like the movies either. All I felt was — thrills, chills, excitement! Nothing like this has ever happened to me before, I wonder what's going to happen next. But you know, the boy of the hour had told me a few days before to wear my seat belt—not in a pushy way did he say it but nicely with simple concern. I must admit for a few seconds in which I couldn't unfasten the damn thing I doubted the wisdom of it but then I shimmied out, squeezing myself small within the circle of safety. And I stood up. And my legs worked. And I wasn't even bleeding or anything and there were red lights of cars and I could see people and I yelled hey hey and tromped over.

The first thing I said was, "Man, I have to be onstage at Lollapalooza tomorrow, I can't believe I did this, how'm I gonna get there?" It was a car full of kids on their way to the show and they had honked at me because of Louise's paint job. She's one of those Tom Cramer cars—you know, you've seen them. She looked like an exotic insect on its back there in the dark. We scared a coyote, too, he peered bright-eyed through the bushes and the guy told the girls just get back in the car. They went over the hill for the cell phone to work to summon the law and left me with Monty. They did not come back to give me a ride.

Monty. The out-of-work trucker with a borrowed car and a pinched nerve in his arm. His wife left him and his girlfriend (whose CB handle is "Wacky") has cancer. Monty knows about the big C 'cause it took his grandma and he's on anti-depressants now and lives at mile marker 42. He drives around looking for accidents so he can help and he's gonna run for CB club president come December. I said to him, "Monty, you're a walking country song," while I sipped Wacky's Pepsi and sat beside the supper he was taking to her and watched it get cold. Monty's doctor told him country's the worst thing for depression; well, I can't argue with that. I did remember the wine bottle from the picnic with you-know-who and I chucked it into coyote's living room as far as I could before the state trooper arrived.

He did come, after a long rural time and then so did the tow truck and man it was hard watching Junior flip her back overhearing those groaning crunches in reverse and wondering why am i even standing here? She's an ill-fated celebrity, that Louise. Her 15 seconds of fame in that flop Cowgirls movie and then the rock show did her in. It's funny. But I had my copy of *Catcher in the Rye* with me, my new Uncle Tupelo t-shirt, some stuff from the X-Ray yard sale (including Ben's sign that said "I hope I'm as cool as her"). Yeah, funny, all right. I lost my toothbrush but found the toothpaste in the dirt. So, thanks to the state trooper for being so nice, calling ahead to find the inn that had room and delivering me. And he didn't double the fine like he should have cause it was a construction zone — Yeah! You know, you have to pay for anything when the law comes — even if no one and nothing is hurt and no way can you just leave your car there. (Monty was adamant about this, and he's seen a lot.) Good luck!—to the state trooper's wife. She's a hairdresser like me but can't make enough to cover daycare in Yakima. Too much competition. Thanks to the night clerk who arranged for a cab without blinking a sleepy eye. I set the hotel alarm clock for 7, cab comes, go to cash machine, card expired: it's the first day of September. Just barely. I cry in the back seat and he takes the big check for the big fare.

You might say, why didn't I just hitch, or bail out, how crazy to spend 150 bucks to cruise through the Saddle Mountains in a lime green '74 Impala (this engine sure is hesitating, darlin') hearing about the cabbie's childhood in Arkansas, his musical family, his years in the service and he loves rock and roll — Clapton, Zeppelin— why, he's taken fares to Tacoma and back—but this check had better be good Jennifer and how come you never got married? We pull up to the site in a cloud of dust and he peels out in another one. See, everyone reacts the way that they do—anyway my different drummer said to get to the gig, get there on time and get there safe no matter what it takes and the easiest way out is almost always money. Just ask Ben and Tres.

So yeah, I read my poem about X-Ray for the slam. I preached the gospel of 2nd & Burnside to the wayward alternative children of Washington with wildly shaking sheets of paper in my crazy nervous hand. I really did know it by heart— but when I had sat a few hours before in the hotel room—in shock—towel over my head and all my belongings lined up in front of me in a row on the floor— when I sat there—I couldn't even say "quit talking and start chalking"—could picture the pinball machine okay but the words wouldn't get from behind my teeth. Anyways, I slammed, and did the open mikes and saw the monks, and met this one completely cool, real live poet named Neal. A lot of people might write poems, but almost none of us, me neither, are actually the spirit holders, the watchers, the soul revealers—poets. This Neal, he's Chief Joseph's child— from Vancouver B.C. with MAИ branded between his shoulder blades.

He intones this angry sad prayer of gasoline genocide, turning into a warrior, rocking the mike stand and staring wild and true. When he finished, he slunk off like a sullen gas station attendant. Magic.

There was some of that, a little, and plenty of ranting—empty political rants, feminist and male sexist rants, suicidal, necrophiliac and weird personal rants. It seemed I'd heard the same poems before from other people—like we're all thinking the same thing. All kinds of talking on the Revival Stage. I think we all felt a little bit giddy and a little bit silly and maybe some of us thought we were rock stars.

During the slam, I was keeping count, waiting my turn, so I knew when it was the guy before me and he was this nerdy computer geek death rocker. Just imagine. I was dreading following his mosquito drone plea for us all to just "kill ourselves now" (of course he introduced it with reference to Kurt Cobain and assured us he didn't really mean it which to me says why say it then, but...)

225

So, I'm waiting for my name to be called when this hippie-looking fellow in a sarong skirt and nothing else takes the mike to whimper that he's really upset with that security guard ...man... who says it's not cool for me to wear a skirt and ...snuffle snuffle... I don't have any other clothes and that's... JUST NOT COOL!! The drag queen named Torment (wearing a minidress made of 3,000 tortoise shell fender guitar picks) takes the mike from the disgruntled hippie to explode about anyone's right to wear whatever they want, I'm calling your supervisor, mister, and you've just learned a valuable lesson — do not ever fuck with the DRAG QUEEN!

This, I have to follow? Oy! I got up there and did my best—and the funny thing is that the message of the X-ray poem is how it was really almost impossible to feel dumb there—that place had a charm of some kind. Not that fights never happened—but just what a difference between the big testosterone charged concert in the field—I never saw so many frat punk boys! Oh well. Before anyone else came in—the poets met under a tent to go over the schedule and introduce ourselves. So, we're passing the mike around the circle—some people talking about the books they've published and some just saying their name, age and sign (like Saturday afterhours with Dave Queen!). This one girl said "I write to live!" and I said that I was a hairdresser and I just made things up so I could have an excuse to be onstage and be a ham. While everyone laughed and applauded my honesty, I had to think too, about that writing to live.

See, this boy, he wonders about when people use a big event to make new art—like do you use misfortune to fuel your muse or exploit sad or scary things for the good story to tell at parties. It's a good question... maybe the truth is we live to write. And a zine is just a public journal.

But... it did cost me 10 times as much as anyone else to get into Lollapalooza for free, and it does make a good story—and sometimes you can't measure the worth of things that don't compare at all.

I played rock star for a day, wearing my patch over the huge brake fluid stain on my '30s slip dress (cool!). I lost my one and only beautiful bus, but I don't have to pay car insurance anymore. I'll sell the motor to pay for towing her back—it all evens out. Louise will get to be a playhouse for Vanessa's kids, and I end up alone still, I think. In one week a lot can change. You might walk away from a car wreck, but that doesn't mean you're not damaged. You might walk away from love if you can stand up after falling—it all just comes and goes, I guess.

# In Conclusion...

## Manifest Destiny

Dominique Lowell
San Francisco California

To seek to know To Know. To strip Maya of her veil and nuns of
their habits. Caprice has a notion don't get in her way. She's
a wild thaaaaaaang with a freewheeling flurry of cobwebs in her
wake. With a pop and a toss she chucks morals like old beercans
in the wastebasket.
M-O-R-A-L-I-T-Y?
Cogent constrained chinese water torture of oppression. No black
no white just grey tight skirts of Behaviour strained through old
cheesecloth. Crumpled old soldiers who rest their wormy limp
pricks on velvet hemorrhoid cushions while they machinate the
dissection of souls. With a digital watch.
Time is the greatest whip of oppression. It can be used from any
distance. A torpid touch, the slightest glance, and we dance a
cold measured step in the middle of the road. Granular, and
carefully glazed.
Well no. None of that. I worship only whimsy!
All levers and lubricants needed to pry a last bit of suffocating
soul from grey bondage shall be used to excess. A fulmination of
excess is the prescription. Salve of extremity, balm of
nonsense, cool cloth of waywardness. To be as bad as it takes to
be a true saint. A true seeker. To seek to know To Know and no
cold feet allowed.
Pregnant with lust for the unknown, divine the gurgles and
murmurs of chaotic joy rambling and unraveling through the
abdomen and the chest and the thorax. Well give them no rest.
No time for effete politesse. Play is serious business.
Frivolity ain't no laughing matter.
And Love must be made. Must be found. Must be redefined and
reintroduced to us all. Ripped from the gut and splattered
brutally on the wall. Peals of laughter will splay it through
the streets like a muthafuckin riot.
Because, you see, sheer exuberance is the only responsibility.
Convulsive
and naked.

## The Wonderful World of Horses

Gary Glazner
San Francisco California

Ladies and Gentlemen the Royal Lipizzaner Stallions
doing the Pas de Deux, crab walking sideways louie.
Amazing, fantastic, awesome, saved by General
Patton, as seen in the Disney movie, they jump, they kick,
they fly through the air with the greatest of
way fucking cool ease.
The royal Lollapalooza horse poets,
the spam eating, grape up their butts poets.
Walk, trot, canter, gallop.
Black hats, red coats, all the horses have tattoos
and horse cock, nipple, mane rings.
Check out the bits in their mouths,
Horse in center ring, drooling, slobbering, white spit
shooting out of pony stallion horsey mouth.
But that's good, in some competitions judges grade lower
for horses that don't slobber. When a horse slobbers it means
he's accepted the bit, working it and comfortable.
Foaming at the mouth Lollapalooza horse poets.
Bred centuries just for this moment.
We've got to train our horses with heart and soul
not just physical strength.
He knows you're applauding and he likes it.
Horse waves hoof, crowd goes wild.
Dancing poet stallions of Vienna.
When General Patton heard the Royal Lollapalooza poets
were being held by the Beastie Boys,
he ordered everybody's pants to be worn at half mast.
Hopped in his tank, cruised over to the poetry tent,
and opened fire, cannon blasting Brady Bunch bombs.
Horses tap-dancing into your hearts.
Kenneth Rexroth on the second stage,
on top of Robert Duncan.
There goes Emily Dickinson on her mount Bukowski,
whipping him into a riding crop frenzy.
Ladies and gentlemen, it's the royal Lipizzaner/ Lollapalooza
poetry stallions for your pleasure, for your love.
Doing it for you all day long.
Poetry horse meat, taste just like chicken
Step right up, it's good for you,
you are going to love this flesh.

## Sonic Amplification

Mud Baron
Glendale California

poetry karaoke    p-mud wrastlin,  fast food poetry  game show poetry, russian roulette poetry   satanic back trackin po'   muzak poe   poet assault vehicle PAV p's armed  with  sonic  amplification          deeeeevices          nakedp meateatinfeetsmellinpoetry  groupsexword   my city's on fire   where i am p. drug induced p.    male vs. female p oetry   asshole poets   sassy magazine poetry    who-do-you-hate-more-than-anyone-in-the-world-words    damaged by jesus, et al.  poetrynice treesand bigrockpoetry  i hate my parents po    i'm in lust luv poetmy job sucks a big one   sucking the big one p    authority sucks poe    i'm insane word/everyone but me is  wordgrocery store top10authors suck and so do yuppies, hippies, assholes, penises, cunts, other parts and my job too poetry    what kind of poetry showd i read ah hooooow to reeeed it flute boy at palooooooo nipple pierce bad tattoo 8track rok sho   blew the band alienabductednation  conspiracy of the inane  roadstory chicken ranching garlic dayjob while i raked blueberry poptarts in maine one summer and julie from the squat pooped out of the port o potty in the middle of a field outside of a field down east is often a surprise

LOLLAPALOOZA 1994

REVIVAL

MindField Day Pass

## Editors' Thanks

The Editors wish to thank everyone who checked out the Spoken Word scene at Lollapalooza '94; all the poets, writers, and performers who participated; the local poet coordinators; and Perry Farrell, Ted Gardener, Nikki Brown, and the producers of Lollapalooza for making the Revival Tent a success.

Special thanks and acknowledgments: Donita Sparks, Jennifer Finch, Suzi Gardener, Dee Plakas, Brubaker, Paul Bearer, Bam Bam, Michael Diamond, the Beastie Boys, Angelo Moore, the Breeders, Stereolab, Flaming Lips, Pharcyde, John Rubeli, Gorby, Subliminal Islam, Billy Corgan, Torment, John Sinclair, Ray Manzarek, Michael McClure, Barry Haney, the Monk Butlers, Rhonda Kennedy, Eve Zamora, Kim Griess, Dan Choi, Eric Humbert, Shawn London, Wiley, Ed McGinty, Troy Herron, Felicia Villareal, Renee Horiuchi, Rock for Choice, the Last Poets, the Watts Prophets, Boom Poetics, DFL, Gary at 2.13.61, Manic D Press, all the poets, our local coordinators, and everyone who helped make the Revival Tent happen. It was fun.

# Acknowledgments

Grateful acknowledgment is made to the authors in this book for permission to print and/or reprint their works, many of which were originally published in unique limited editions, produced by the authors themselves.

We also wish to acknowledge the following presses and individuals for giving us permission to reprint the following:

"Bad Day at the Beauty Salon" by Maggie Estep from *No More Mister Nice Girl* (NuYo Records). Copyright ©1994. Reprinted by permission of the author.

"56 Reasons To Go Downtown" by Iris Berry from *Two Blocks East of Vine*. Copyright ©1994. Reprinted by permission of Incommunicado Press.

"La Letty" by Michele Serros from *Chicana Falsa* (Lalo Press). Copyright ©1993. Reprinted by permission of the author.

"Cigarette Mapping" by Golda Fried from *Oralpalooza '94 Montreal* (Ga Press). Copyright ©1994. Reprinted by permission of the author.

"Better Left Unsaid" by Wendy-o Matik from *Love Like Rage*. Copyright ©1994. Reprinted by permission of Manic D Press.

"Kérosène" by Martin-Pierre Tremblay from *Oralpalooza '94 Montreal* (Ga Press). Copyright ©1994. Reprinted by permission of the author.

"Fly" by Natalie Jacobson from *Emeralds in the Ash*. Copyright ©1994. Reprinted by permission of Raging Muse Press.

"The Hudson Wakes You Up Each Morning" by Regie Cabico from *The Petting Zoo*. Copyright ©1994. Reprinted by permission of the author.

"I Love a Woman Who Eats Animals" by Kevin Sampsell from *How To Lose Your Mind With The Lights On* (Future Tense Press) Copyright © 1994. Reprinted by permission of the author.

"Locks and Keys" by Crisa from *Pieces of a Black Mind* (Sunpress) Copyright ©1994. Reprinted by permission of the author.

"My Country, My Cunt" by Liz Belile from *Polishing The Bayonet*. Copyright ©1994. Reprinted by permission of Incommunicado Press.

"The Body Politic" by Richard Loranger from *The Orange Book* (International Review Press). Copyright ©1990. Reprinted by permission of the author.

"If We Only Knew" by Abiodun Oyewole from *Selected Poems: The Last Poets*. Copyright ©1993. Reprinted by permission of the author.

"Dispose of the Monster" by Angelo Moore from *Dr. Madd Vibe's Comprehensive Linkology*. Copyright ©1994. Reprinted by permission of the author.

"Information" by Tricia Warden from *Brainlift*. Copyright ©1994. Reprinted by permission of 2.13.61.

"Maybe Mama Lion" by Michael McClure from *Rebel Lions*. Copyright ©1994. Reprinted by permission of New Directions.

"Mission District Late Night" by George Tirado from *The Final Observations of a Technoshaman*. Copyright ©1994. Reprinted by permission of Road Kill Press.

"How I Am Defined By American Heritage" by Laurie Conner from *Emeralds in the Ash, Vol. 1 No. 4*. Copyright ©1994. Reprinted by permission of Raging Muse Press.

"Twentynothing" by Jeff McDaniel from *Alibi School* Copyright ©1995. Reprinted by permission of Manic D Press.

"Lousy Neighbors" by Jon Longhi from *The Rise and Fall of Third Leg*. Copyright ©1994. Reprinted by permission of Manic D Press.

"Divine Symphony of the Damned" by Bucky Sinister from *King of the Roadkills*. Copyright ©1995. Reprinted by permission of Manic D Press.

"She Was So Bad" by Pleasant Gehman from *Senorita Sin*. Copyright ©1994. Reprinted by permission of Incommunicado Press.

"Manifest Destiny" by Dominique Lowell from *Pile*. Copyright © 1991. Reprinted by permission of Grace Street Press.

# Manic D Press
## publications


Revival: spoken word from Lollapalooza 94.
>> *edited by Juliette Torrez, Liz Belile, Mud Baron*
>> *& Jennifer Joseph.* $12.95

The Ghastly Ones & Other Fiendish Frolics. *Richard Sala.* $9.95

The Underground Guide to San Francisco.
>> *edited by Jennifer Joseph.* $10.95

King of the Roadkills. *Bucky Sinister.* $9.95

Alibi School. *Jeffrey McDaniel.* $8.95

Signs of Life: channel-surfing through '90s culture.
>> *edited by Jennifer Joseph & Lisa Taplin.* $12.95

Beyond Definition: new writing from gay & lesbian san francisco.
>> *edited by Marci Blackman & Trebor Healey.* $10.95

Love Like Rage. *Wendy-o Matik* $7.00

The Language of Birds. *Kimi Sugioka* $7.00

The Rise and Fall of Third Leg. *Jon Longhi* $9.95

Specimen Tank. *Buzz Callaway* $10.95

The Verdict Is In.
>> *edited by Kathi Georges & Jennifer Joseph* $9.95

Elegy for the Old Stud. *David West* $7.00

The Back of a Spoon. *Jack Hirschman* $7.00

Mobius Stripper. *Bana Witt* $8.95

Baroque Outhouse / The Decapitated Head of a Dog.
>> *Randolph Nae* $7.00

Graveyard Golf and other stories. *Vampyre Mike Kassel* $7.95

Bricks and Anchors. *Jon Longhi*  $8.00
The Devil Won't Let Me In. *Alice Olds-Ellingson*  $7.95
Greatest Hits. *edited by Jennifer Joseph* $7.00
Lizards Again. *David Jewell* $7.00
The Future Isn't What It Used To Be. *Jennifer Joseph* $7.00
Acts of Submission. *Joie Cook* $4.00
Zucchini and other stories. *Jon Longhi* $3.00
Standing In Line. *Jerry D. Miley* $3.00
Drugs. *Jennifer Joseph* $3.00
Bums Eat Shit and other poems. *Sparrow 13* $3.00
Into The Outer World. *David Jewell* $3.00
Solitary Traveler. *Michele C.* $3.00
Night Is Colder Than Autumn. *Jerry D. Miley*  $3.00
Seven Dollar Shoes. *Sparrow 13 LaughingWand.* $3.00
Intertwine. *Jennifer Joseph* $3.00
Feminine Resistance. *Carol Cavileer* $3.00
Now Hear This. *Lisa Radon.* $3.00
Bodies of Work. *Nancy Depper* $3.00
Corazon Del Barrio. *Jorge Argueta.* $4.00


Please add $2.00 to all orders for postage and handling.

## Manic D Press
## Box 410804
## San Francisco CA 94141 USA


distributed to the trade in the US & Canada by
publishers group west